PASSIVE INCOME - 10 WAYS TO GENERATE
A PASSIVE INCOME STREAM WITH
OFFLINE BUSINESSES

CONTENTS

INTRODUCTION

Who does not want to achieve financial freedom and have an unlimited earning potential? Passive income is the answer to your financial woes. With this kind of income, you can live the life that you have always dreamed of.

Going to work and receiving a paycheck every month is good because it allows you to pay your bills, buy food, and have some money left for savings or personal expenses. However, this amount of money is fixed and limited. It does not give you room for growth.

Even worse, you are tied to your work schedule and stuck in your work desk. You cannot just get up and leave the office. You have to work for eight hours straight every day for five or six days a week.

This problem will not be in existent if you have a passive income. With a passive income, you can be your own boss. You can control your own time and schedule. You get to decide how much money you want to make or how you want to spend your time.

You get to take a nap whenever you want and go on trips out of the country as often as possible. You get to go wherever you want and still earn a good amount of money.

No one would tell you how you should use your time or pressure you to finish a project, task, or office work. You do not have to answer to a supervisor or manager. You do not even have to deal with co-workers.

Having a passive income source lets you be in total control of your financial endeavors. If you are able to monitor or maintain your passive income source online, you can simply take your laptop or tablet with you anytime and anywhere. You can check out the progress of your business whenever and wherever you are.

This kind of freedom is not available to everyone. It is only enjoyed by those who have the guts to take a risk from the safety net of employment and venture out on their own.

Then again, there is really no need for you to give up your job or career. Once you have established your passive income source, you can go back to work if that is what you want to do. Since you have full control of your time, you can go back to your career and earn more money. That is the beauty of having a passive income. You have the option to work or not work as an employee.

In this book, you will read about passive income, what it is, why it is important, and how you can get started with it. You will also learn about the other types of income as well as how they compare to passive income.

More importantly, you will learn about ten ways on how you can earn a passive income. You will learn about their descriptions, pros and cons, and requirements.

Thanks for downloading this book. I hope you enjoy it!

CHAPTER 1

WHAT IS PASSIVE INCOME?

Say, you are a limited partner at your best friend's restaurant. Since the restaurant is located at a busy part of town, near office buildings and universities, it is frequented by customers. This lets you receive a good amount of money regularly.

However, this money is not salary or wage because you do not have to actively manage the business, serve customers, clean, cook, etc. It is passive income. You earn money even if you are away or out of town. You do not even have to go to the establishment every day.

THE BASIC DEFINITION OF PASSIVE INCOME

Passive income is the type of income that is earned from a source that does not involve active work.

Financial Mentor founder and wealth coach Todd Tresidder said that passive income is an income that you get with no regard to your time. Then again, he also emphasized that it is not mailbox money or money that merely shows up.

Passive income is also lagged income. If you want to have it, you have to exert energy and time in the beginning. It is like a machine that you have to build first in order to make it work for you, even if you do not manually operate it.

Interest and dividends can also be regarded as passive income. As a taxpayer, you have to fill out an IRS Schedule C, D, E, or F to report your passive income.

The Different Types of Income

Now, before we tackle passive income further, it is vital for you to learn about the other types of income that exist. In essence, there are three primary types of income:

a. passive income

b. earned income

c. portfolio income

Any money that you earn would fall into one of these categories, except if you receive an inheritance or win the lottery. Every one of these categories has its own pros and cons.

Passive Income

This is the money that you get from any asset that you have created or purchased. So, if you purchase a house and then rent it out, you can earn enough money to pay the mortgage plus other expenses, provided that you charge a rental fee that is higher than the price you bought the house for.

Another example is if you have a business that can operate independently, you can earn a passive income from it. If you leave this business alone for a few days, weeks, or months, it will still run and make money. However, if this business requires that you put in a certain number of hours and you will not make any money unless you complete these hours then this business does not produce passive income. Instead, it produces earned income.

Some of the activities that can give you a passive income include business income that is not made based on the amount of effort and/or time spent, rental income or real estate income, multi-level or affiliate marketing, and creating and selling of intellectual properties, such as books, web content, and patents.

With this being said, you can tell that there are a lot of benefits to passive income over any other types of income. For starters, passive income is recurring. After you have made your investment, you can expect a continuous flow of money. Of course, this would only happen if your investment is a good one. The money you will receive will go on for months, years, or even decades.

Once you have exerted the effort necessary, you can sit back and relax as you wait for your passive income to arrive on a regular basis. You can even consider yourself as retired while still growing your net worth. There are so many things you can do with your free time.

The investments that result in a passive income typically let the owners actively control them. For instance, if you have a corporation or apartment building, you have the right to meddle with the operations that will ultimately affect the success of such investment.

More often than not, the investments that yield a passive income lead to favorable tax treatments. Companies and corporations may use the profits to make investments in other sources or opportunities. For instance, they may use their earnings to purchase real estate and consequently, earn another passive income from it.

In addition, they can benefit from the tax deductions that come along with this investment. Real estate may even be traded for a bigger property, with the taxes deferred indefinitely.

Since it is usually possible to approximate returns closely, you may fund your investments with borrowed money. Say, you have a great business plan. You can ask other people to invest in the business. You may even attract venture capital money or angel funding.

Real estate may also be obtained using a small down payment. Usually, individuals who wish to purchase real estate are only asked to give a twenty percent down payment of the total amount.

Hence, you can really see that passive income is key to generating long term wealth. If you want to be rich, you should aim to have multiple passive income sources.

THE PROS AND CONS OF PASSIVE INCOME

Having a passive income is the dream of most people. It really has a lot of benefits. Then again, it also comes with certain drawbacks. It is important for you to understand the pros and cons associated with this type of income before you invest in anything. This way, you would be properly informed.

The Pros:

Multiple Income Streams

One really good thing about passive income is that you may easily have two or more income streams. For example, you can create an e-book to serve as a study guide for students about to take an exam. Then, you can also create a blog wherein you upload articles that are relevant to the content of your e-book. In this blog, you can talk about topics that can help students prepare and pass their exams.

Afterwards, you can also set up a membership website and encourage your existing blog followers or e-book customers to subscribe. Once they sign up, you can send them newsletters and updates regarding promos and special offers. You can sell more e-books or other products that are relevant to your niche. There are so many possibilities. You just have to be creative and have an open mind.

More Free Time

This is what a lot of people want to have in their lives. They want to have more time for themselves, for their family, for their friends, for their partner, etc. They want to be able to do great things aside from work or deal with business matters.

When you have a passive income, you can easily take a day off to go on a local vacation or a trip abroad. You can start a new hobby or enroll in a course. You can also pamper yourself and get a good massage.

With more free time, you will be able to take better care of yourself. You can prepare and cook nutritious meals at home, go to the gym, and sleep longer. You can rest, take a break, and enjoy the good things in life without worrying about money or work.

Schedule Flexibility

This is similar to having more free time. When you have a flexible schedule, you can begin and end your work however you wish. For example, you can open your boutique at 10 AM and close it at 2 PM. You can even choose not to open it at all if you want to take a day off.

Unlike with employment or a job, you do not have to come in at exactly 8 o'clock in the morning. There is no need for you to stay out late because your boss tells you to work overtime. You do not have to eat your lunch in a hurry because you can have a long lunch break if you want to.

You can even take your children to work. If you are a parent and are worried about leaving your children in the care of someone else or you simply want to spend more time with them, you can take them to your place of business. Likewise, you can hang out with your friends at your shop and earn money as you have a fun time.

More Financial Security

Since you can have multiple income streams, you can also have more money. This would give you an increased financial security because you do not have to depend on just one source of income.

With employment or a day job, you may constantly worry about getting fired or laid off. If you lose your job, you also lose your source of income. This would mean that you will no longer be able to afford paying for rent, buying food, and paying for other necessities.

If, for some unexpected reason, your income is suddenly cut off, you will have a lot of problems. With passive income and multiple income streams, you always have a backup plan. If something goes wrong with a source of income, you still have other sources to turn to.

The Cons:

Low Starting Income

This can be a huge problem if you have a lot of expenses or do not have anyone else to turn to for help in case you experience a financial crisis. At first, you need to exert a lot of time and effort to build your business or passive income source. You have to establish and make it grow. You have to face all the challenges that will come along as you make yourself to the top.

It is important for you to be adequately prepared for these challenges. A lot of people actually quit before they even get to the middle of their journey. They do not have the capacity to deal with such challenges. They lose hope when they lose money and do not see profits. They allow their doubts to overpower them. They choose to go back to a safer way to earn money, which is usually earned income.

As you know, business ventures and passive income sources do not guarantee success. You may either fail or succeed in your chosen venture. Then again, passive income products typically have exponential growth. This means that they would give you good returns in the long run, provided that you stick with them and make sure that you learn how to grow them.

Not Enough Socialization

If social life is important for you, you may have a hard time adjusting to the lifestyle associated with earning a passive income. Since you are not in a typical office setting, you will not have co-workers that you can constantly chat and hang out with. You have to get out there and seek new friends. You can attend social events, for example, if you want to meet people.

There would be times when you will feel isolated. This is especially true in the beginning when you are just starting to figure out how to establish and operate your passive income source. You may not see and interact with a lot of people. So, you should make it a point to socialize with family and friends at least every weekend.

Success Is Not Guaranteed

No matter how much you research and how hard you work, you still cannot have a 100% guarantee that you will succeed in your chosen passive income venture. This is why you have to prepare yourself physically, mentally, and emotionally. You have to understand that you can lose everything if you make a wrong move.

For example, you can spend months setting up your blog. You do your research and spend time writing informative articles. However, this would not guarantee that people will visit your site and read your blog. Likewise, you can buy expensive camera equipment and shoot videos on a daily basis for your YouTube channel. However, you still cannot guarantee that people will subscribe and watch your vlogs.

If you make a little money at first, this is not a guarantee that you will continue making money. You also have to consider if the money you are making is enough to support yourself. If you notice that you are losing more money than you are making or if you still have not gotten back the money that you spent initially, then perhaps you are in the wrong field.

Also, even if you already make a good reputation for yourself, you still cannot be certain that your subscribers will continue patronizing your work. An unexpected thing might happen, such as having a misunderstanding or a fight with a major brand. This can ultimately destroy your reputation and your career.

EARNED INCOME

This is the type of income that you get from the labor you produce. In other words, it is earned by working. People who have this kind of income usually receive an hourly income or salary. They typically work from their own consulting or for someone else.

Some of the activities that result in earned income include consulting, working a job, gambling, operating a small business, and any other task that pays based on effort or time spent.

Earned income is actually the most typical means for earning money. However, it is not the most ideal. The moment you stop working or exerting effort, you also stop earning money.

Moreover, since the amount of money that you can make from this type of income is directly proportional to the effort and time you spend working, you can have a hard time making more of it if you do not have the necessary skills.

If you want to earn more money, you have to learn new skills; and you cannot do this if you have to render a specific number of hours to your job. The only thing you can do to make more money with this type of income is to work longer hours or overtime.

Earned income also comes with the highest taxes. Nonetheless, a significant benefit you can get from it is that you do not have to shell out a startup capital if you want to earn it. You just have to go out there and start working. For example, you can seek employment at a company or sell food on the streets.

Earned income is quite easy to get, which is why most people depend on it. Most students, for example, would immediately look for a job after graduating from college. A lot of businessmen also had to work jobs to save money for their business funding.

With this being said, you can conclude that earned income is a good way to begin your investing goals. It would let you save up enough money to help start your own business or establish another type of income.

The Pros and Cons of Earned Income

Earned income is also commonly referred to as business spin-off, enterprise endeavor, for-profit undertaking, entrepreneurial activity, profit-making operation, and commercialism. Whatever you choose to call it, earned income is a great way for non-profits to gain funding.

You can earn this type of income by taking a workshop and finding out how to make money from it. You can expand its current scope or conduct a survey and find out what clients want in a service or product. Then, give these paying clients what they want.

If you have decided that you want to engage in earned income opportunities, it is only proper for you to learn about its pros and cons.

The Pros:

Money Usage Freedom

You have the freedom to do whatever you want with your money since there aren't any strings attached. If you want to spend all of your salary in one week, then you can go ahead and do that. If you want to put it in a bank account or an investment opportunity, you can do that as well.

Encourages Independence

Since you have to work for your money, you learn how to become independent. You learn that you cannot depend on anyone else but yourself. You cannot be lazy and irresponsible with your finances and work. Otherwise, you may lose your job and not be able to pay for the things you need. You may also not be able to find a new job if you have a bad reputation or work history.

Organization Improvement

Your organization or company can grow stronger when it has a diverse set of offerings. In addition, this type of income can help improve the visibility and image of your organization.

Promotes Better Customer Relations

If you want to keep your job or continue having customers and clients, you have to have a good attitude. You need to build rapport with these people as well as learn how to deal even with the most difficult ones. Wanting to keep a job or small business can be sufficient motivation for you to improve your relations with other people.

The Cons:

Time-Consuming

Market research can be extensive. Aside from this, you also have to create a business plan as well as prepare financial projections. All of these tasks can take a huge amount of your time and energy. However, they are necessary if you want to make earned income work positively for you.

May Need to Educate Others

If you work with a team, you may need to educate them about the nature of the business or job as well. You may need to teach your staff and board members about earned income, including its advantages. In essence, you have to convince and encourage everyone to be committed to your cause.

Risk for Make or Break

The quality of your management can either make or break your venture. Thus, you need to work with the best people. Of course, you also have to pay them rightfully. More often than not, you may have to produce the money upfront.

If you cannot produce cash, you should at least be able to get a loan immediately. This way, you can pay for everything right on schedule. Having a financial backup plan is always necessary if you want to avoid being taken over by the inevitable down turns on the market.

Pointers to Keep In Mind for Earned Income

If you want to succeed in your earned income venture, you have to be prepared to take risks. As much as possible, you have to execute a risk-taking assessment before you even begin this venture.

Also, you have to calculate your risks. Make decisions quickly but carefully. Remember that you should not take more than ninety days to come up with a decision.

Since funding is essential, you also have to establish and maintain a good relationship with bankers. Always pay your loans on time. Do your best to have an excellent credit standing. This way, you will not have a problem acquiring loans or doing other financial transactions.

Aside from having a good relationship with bankers, you also have to have a good relationship with customers or clients. After all, they are the blood line of any business. Without paying customers or clients, businesses will not survive.

You have to give what these people want. You have to be very responsive to them too. Learn about total quality management principles and develop mechanisms for polling customers.

It is also important for you to study your objectives carefully. Know, define, and understand your goals. Do not just focus on making profits. Make it a point to earn enough profits that justify the effort and time that you have spent.

In addition, you must choose fewer ventures with huge payoffs over a lot of ventures with small returns. It is much easier to monitor and handle ventures when there are only a few of them. Since they have high returns, you will not feel the need to start other ventures that may only have small returns.

Furthermore, see to it that your venture makes the most of your expertise, program strengths, and staff time. Do not forget to keep an eye out on the marketplace. Prepare yourself to quickly adapt to anything that might arise in this fast-moving and constantly evolving world.

PORTFOLIO INCOME

This type of income is made by selling investments at much higher prices than you bought them for. It is sometimes referred to as capital gain since it is how the federal government taxes the money from it.

It is important to keep in mind that portfolio income is not produced by passive income investments. It is also not earned by doing regular business activities.

Some of the activities that typically lead to portfolio income include buying and selling real estate, buying and selling other assets such as cars, antiques, and collectibles, and buying and/or selling paper assets. You can trade paper assets such as stocks, mutual funds, bonds, ETF's, T-bills, CD's, currencies, and other types of futures or derivatives. You can also trade in the stock market.

Then again, you have to have the right knowledge to make this type of income work for you. Portfolio income is not for everyone. This is why a lot of people lose money when trading stocks. They do not understand the market well or do not have enough knowledge about the products.

Keep in mind that you need to exert enough time and effort to learn the ways of trading paper assets. You have to learn how to analyze trends in the market and read financial statements. You also have to research about the companies that you want to be involved with.

More often than not, you will also not have a lot of control over your investments. It is basically like gambling. You can only buy and sell, but you cannot know for certain what you will get. Even if you study the market and analyze the odds carefully, you still cannot be 100% sure of the outcome.

Say, you want to purchase some stocks in a company. If you do this, you will be able to have a daily control of its operations. However, you will also not have enough time to control your investments on a daily basis.

In addition, you need to invest the money immediately. You need to present these funds upfront. Take note that even huge gains are not consequential if the investing amount is too small.

Your portfolio income will also be taxed at a very high rate. In a lot of cases, this income is equal to earned income. Nevertheless, once you sharpen your knowledge and skills, this type of income will certainly work well for you in the long run.

You can reinvest after every sale. If you hold your portfolio assets for a long period of time, you will also be able to enjoy lower tax rates.

The Pros and Cons of Portfolio Income

Whether you invest in bonds, stocks, or any other sources of portfolio income, you need to make sure that you know what to do in order to maximize your total returns. Studying the pros and cons of this type of income is a good start.

The Pros:
Great Asset Classes

Investing in portfolio income sources can give you low correlations with other investments and excellent returns. You can also take advantage of the various ways on how to decrease its active aspect. What's more, you can easily use these sources to increase your portfolio leverage.

Entrepreneurship Opportunities

You can easily add value, expertise, and work to your investments. You may also realize that investing in individual income properties is worthwhile.

Amazing Total Returns

There is no more need for you to dread retirement. You can enjoy high-income investments with good total returns. Even if portfolio income sources do not completely guarantee financial success, you can have a high chance of succeeding if you are risk tolerant within reason. You can benefit from the solid total returns as well as the low correlation with stocks.

Freedom to Leverage Other Investments

There are plenty of ways on how you can leverage your stock market investments. You may even borrow against real estate if necessary.

The Cons:
High Yields Do Not Mean High Returns

You have to know early on that high yields do not exactly mean high returns. Say, you want cash flow. You can get a ten percent cash flow. You can give $100 and get $10 per year for the next ten years.

In case you do not get anything back after this timeframe, you may not think that your investment was good. However, you should always consider the total return, even though you are an "income investor".

Higher Risk and Leverage Plus More Work and Expertise Are Necessary for Higher Returns

Publicly traded companies can actually produce a 7% return annually. In fact, real estate investors can receive much higher returns. But what is really needed to get these high returns?

For starters, you have to take more risks. If you want to gain more rewards, you have to be open to more possibilities. For instance, you can expect a 4% to 10% nominal return from a real estate property that is not leveraged. You can also expect an additional appreciation rate, which usually tracks inflation.

Then again, when you apply leverage, you can expect a higher return. So, if you have a 9% unleveraged return, you can have a higher leveraged return depending on your credit cost. Say, you have a 5% loan on 2/3 of its value. If this is the case, you can have a 16.5% leveraged return, minus the transaction costs.

Some Investors May Not Use a Retirement Account

When you become a professional investor, you can invest in retirement accounts such as Roth IRA's and 401(k)'s. Do not be like the real estate investors who ignore such benefit.

You need to have a retirement account that can help increase your investment return, simplify estate planning and provide a high level of asset protection. You may still invest in real estate asset classes if you want.

Working Too Long and Dying with Too Much

It is unfortunate that some income investors or portfolio income earners work too long and die with too much. While planning for your retirement is good, you also have to use your time wisely. It is not advisable to spend all of your time trying to make more money than you will ever need in your lifetime.

Money Is Replaceable or Fungible

You can buy and sell income property, mutual funds, and stocks anytime you want. Money is really fungible, even though there are transaction costs involved. You are not limited to a single way of investing.

The Importance of Passive Income

Passive income is an excellent way to create wealth and save up for retirement. Then again, the tax treatment it receives is different from that of wages. At times, taxpayers attempt to construe their income as passive income in order to deduct any losses that are associated with it. You have to keep in mind that passive loss can only be deductible in an amount that is the same as passive income.

When you have a passive income, you have financial freedom. You do not have to worry about not making any money on a day when you do not work. The amount of money you earn is also not limited to any amount. Unlike with a job, you get a fixed salary. You get the same amount of money, no matter how much effort you exert or how good your skills are.

With passive income streams, you have the opportunity to earn as much money as you want. This, of course, depends on how high your skill levels are. You also have to spend a considerable amount of time in the beginning to build your passive income source. Likewise, you have to periodically check this source to ensure that everything is working exactly the way it should.

Passive income also gives you time freedom. You get to use your time for things that you like. You can travel with your family or friends. You can take up a new hobby or enroll in courses that can help you improve yourself. Since your schedule is flexible, you can do anything you want.

With this being said, a passive income helps you avoid being a slave to money. When you are confident that you have money coming up, you do not obsess about working for it. You take care of your health by getting sufficient amounts of rest and sleep, instead of staying up late every night to work.

Passive income gives you financial security. Yes, it can be risky when you first establish it. As time goes by, however, you realize that it is steady and reliable. It is secure because it is neither connected nor dependent on your time.

Say, your child becomes sick and you have to take care of him. You cannot go to work because you have to take him to the doctor, buy medicine, cook meals, and monitor his condition.

If you have a passive income, this situation will not have a huge impact on your finances. Even if you are not able to go to work, you can still have money to spend on doctor's appointments and medication.

With a passive income, you have a better chance of having a nice and stable future.

How to Earn a Passive Income

The possibilities associated with a passive income are endless. There are plenty of available passive income sources both online and offline. In fact, you can turn online opportunities into offline ones.

Since this book promises to let you learn about the offline passive income opportunities, here are some steps that you can follow. They would help you achieve your financial goals.

However, the following steps should only serve as a guideline to help you get an idea as well as get started on earning a passive income. Do not limit yourself when it comes to opportunities.

Step 1. Choose a passive income source

Determine what you want, what you need, or what you are good at and then base your decision on it. Choose an idea that best fits your own situation. You may gain inspiration from other people and their experiences, but you have to remember that this is personal. You still have to choose something that is right for you.

For example, you have read somewhere that investing in real estate or dividend stocks is the preferred choice of many businessmen. However, you have little to no understanding about such investments. So, rather than follow their footsteps, you should opt for something that is more apt for your existing skill set.

You can still view their success as inspiration and motivation. You can look up to them and admire their diligence, patience, and other good qualities. You can adopt their work habits and values. However, you do not have to choose the passive income source that they have if it does not suit you well.

Step 2. Set your goals

What do you really want to achieve in the future? What are your short-term and long-term goals? How do you see yourself five, ten, or twenty years from now?

Create a vision and aim to make it happen. Work towards your goals in life. Prepare yourself for the challenges that you might face. Keep in mind that the road to success is not smooth.

Decide what you want to do and create backup plans in case you do not get your desired results the first time. Write down these goals so that you can set physical reminders for yourself.

According to researchers, you actually create a more powerful impact when you write down your goals instead of merely setting them on your mind. Most of the people who solely rely on their memory end up failing.

Step 3. Plan your steps carefully

Once you have made up your mind with regard to the kind of passive income source you want to pursue, you have to plan the steps that you have to take.

Find out how you can move from Point A to Point B. Identify the actions that you have to take as well as how much research you need in order to learn the ropes.

Write down your plans on paper so that you can clearly see what you are about to do and make any changes if necessary. Seeing your plans on paper allows you to go from dreaming to acting in reality.

With persistent and constant action, everything you want would eventually materialize. You will gradually reap the fruits of your labor and live the kind of life that you want. You have to set yourself up for long-term success in order to get there.

Step 4: Have other sources of income

While it is great to have a passive income, you may want to have other sources of income as well. This way, you can truly maximize your money making opportunities.

For example, you can take on freelance work such as writing articles, creating online sources, and tutoring students. You can also take on semi-passive income work such as cooking and selling food.

Also, you should remember that nothing lasts forever. Even though your passive income source gives you a steady supply of money, there may come a time when it can no longer sustain you.

For example, your blog or video blogs may give you a passive income. Years from now, however, new bloggers or video bloggers may outdo you. So, fewer people will read your entries or watch your videos. This would significantly lessen the money that you earn from these passive income sources.

So, you have to be prepared for situations like this. Do not be too complacent with your current financial situation. Since you have a lot of free time now, you have to take advantage of it and make the most of it.

Yes, you can use your free time for trips out of town and abroad. However, you should probably not do this every week or month. Allot some time to work on active and semi-passive income sources to ensure that you stay financially secure for the years to come.

Step 5: Research about successful businessmen and entrepreneurs

Successful business owners and entrepreneurs know the importance of passive income that's why they continue to create and maintain passive income streams. Find out about the techniques that they use. Learn how they configure things such as e-mail scripts and sales funnels for selling products. Study the way they filter and interact with their target audience.

Step 6: Look for a mentor

It is good to learn things on your own. However, it would be better to have an expert teach you more about it. Someone who has the knowledge and experience can help you learn a lot of valuable lessons that you can apply to your own situation.

Hitting stumbling blocks as you go along the way is inevitable. If you only learn from the books, you may not be able to find practical and alternative solutions. Experienced businessmen and entrepreneurs have seen it all. Hence, they can help and guide you on your own journey towards success.

The Difference between Passive Income and Earned Income

Earned income refers to the money that you make when you work. This includes salaries, wages, net earnings, and tips. Long-term disability benefits and strike benefits also belong to this category.

Earned income and unearned income are taxed differently. Unearned income includes annuity payments, retirement account distributions, pension income, capital gains, dividends, interest income, bond interest, stock dividends, alimony, and rental real estate income.

In order for you to make Roth IRA or IRA contributions, you have to generate an earned income. Take note that once you retire and stop working, you will not be able to contribute to your retirement account anymore.

Also, the earned income that you have on your retirement can have a significant effect on your Social Security benefits. So, if you obtain your Social Security before your retirement and you have a lot of earned income, you will experience the Social Security limitations. Some of your benefits would be owed back.

Earned Income Tax

With earned income, you have to pay state and federal income taxes as well as Social Security or Medicare taxes known as OASDI, FICA, and payroll taxes. These payroll taxes are taken out of paychecks automatically.

12.4% of your earned income goes to your Social Security. Half of it would come from you and the other half would come from your employer. If you are self-employed, you have to pay it all by yourself. Nonetheless, 6.2% of this tax is deductible.

In addition, this payroll tax depends on how much earned income you receive up to a specific limit. It is known as earnings cap or benefit and contribution base. In 2018, the dollar limit is $128,400. This amount increased to $132,900 in 2019. This means that any added payroll tax will not be owed on earned income beyond this limitation.

Next, you have Medicare tax, which consists of 2.9% of your wages. You and your employer each pay half of it. Then again, unlike Social Security tax, it does not have an earnings cap. It does not tax you.

Wages and other forms of earned income are subject to this tax. You have to pay the entire 2.9% if you are self-employed. Your Medicare and Social Security benefits are funded by your payroll taxes.

Unearned Income Tax

It is not subject to any payroll taxes. So, this is great news for you. Then again, you have to include your unearned income sources to your Adjusted Gross Income (AGI) calculations when you file your federal income tax.

To find your Adjusted Gross Income, you can check out your 1040 tax form. Interest income from savings accounts, pension payments, and IRA withdrawals are typically taxed at a marginal tax rate. Nevertheless, there are still unearned income types that get taxed at lower rates such as qualified dividends and capital gains.

In order for you to build up your unearned income, you have to start saving money at an early age. Do not worry because this kind of income is exempted from payroll taxes.

Retirees and investors can greatly benefit from this. All pre-tax salary deferral contributions made to pension plans, retirement accounts, and other pre-tax contributions can reduce the amount of state and federal income tax liabilities.

Then again, they cannot lessen your FICA or payroll tax since this tax gets taken out of your gross wages.

Once you retire, you would go from depending on your earned income to depending on your unearned income. Since tax treatments vary according to income sources, it is ideal to always have money coming from different sources.

For instance, you should have tax-deferred accounts such as a 401(k) and IRA, after-tax accounts such as brokerage account investments and savings, and tax-free accounts such as Roth IRA's.

You may also consider self-employment. You can take up a handyman job or start a consulting business. Just be careful not to be caught off-guard by the FICA or payroll tax.

If you choose self-employment, see to it that you hire a reliable tax professional. This way, you can calculate your payroll taxes accurately.

The Basics of Earned Income

This kind of income is very common. In fact, almost every person in the world live on it. If you are an employee, you depend on this income as well. You get it in exchange of your services or labor.

In other words, this kind of income is what you receive when you work as an independent contractor or an employee. If you are employed by a company or business owner, you receive a paycheck on a regular basis. You may receive it bi-weekly or weekly and in a fixed amount.

If this arrangement applies to you, you can expect most of your taxes to be automatically taken out of your paycheck. So, the amount that you receive and take home is already significantly reduced.

Why Passive Income Is Better than Earned Income

As you know, earned income is the income you earn when you run a business or work a full-time job. Passive income, on the other hand, is the income you earn when you rent out property, receive royalties, or have stakes in a limited partnership.

Earned income is associated with high taxes. Hence, it must be used to build wealth quickly. Then again, in order for you to reduce your tax position, you have to move your wealth into portfolio and passive income streams.

Earned income is also subject to your FICA taxes and marginal tax rate. If you want to reduce your tax exposure, you can run an S-corporation, create deductible expenses, and invest in the business. Your net income, however, would still have high effective tax rates.

What is the downside to this?

Well, if you want to reduce your tax exposure with your earned income, you have to spend a lot of money. This is not a practical solution if you have a lot of expenses.

On the other hand, passive income earned from real estate properties is not subject to high effective tax rates. Amortization and depreciation shelter the real estate income. Thus, this leads to lower effective tax rates.

Say, you have a rental property with a net of $10,000 before amortization and depreciation. Likewise, let us say that your amortization and depreciation are $8,000. This gives you a $2,000 net taxable income.

So, if you belong to the 37% tax bracket, you have to pay a $740 tax. If you compare this with the $10,000 amount you earn, you will realize that you have a 7.4% effective tax rate.

What if you earn the same $10,000 as earned income?

If this is the case, you have to spend more money just to reduce your tax. Otherwise, you would be obliged to pay $3,7000 with your $10,000 earned income.

When it comes to real estate, there is no need for you to pay for the depreciation annually. In fact, you get to claim this phantom expense. So when you view things from a tax perspective, you will realize that passive income is much better than earned income.

CHAPTER 2

DIFFERENT WAYS TO GENERATE A
PASSIVE INCOME

As you have read previously, there are plenty of benefits to having a passive income.

Aside from having time and financial flexibility, it would also significantly reduce the stress and anxiety that you may feel towards the future. If you are like most people, you are probably worried about what might happen to you a few months or years from now.

Thinking about not being able to pay bills can truly induce anxiety, stress, and fear. These what-if scenarios can start to take over your mind and negatively affect you physically, mentally, and emotionally.

When you are always fearful of the future, you will find it difficult to live in the present. You will not be able to enjoy what you currently have because you are obsessed about unpleasant possibilities.

However, if you have a passive income, you can alleviate your stress and anxiety. You can relax and be at peace knowing that you have a cushion to fall onto in case you become a casualty of corporate downsizing or lose your job.

When you do not have to worry too much about possible financial problems, you can feel better. This can have a positive impact on your health and wellness. It can make you happier and more productive as well.

Even better, you will feel motivated to start another passive income stream. This is obviously good news because you can have more financial cushions. The more passive income streams you have, the more security you can get.

Another reason why you should make passive income streams a priority is because they can give you a platform for financial growth and stability. If you have an automatic income, there is no need for you to worry about meeting monthly expenses.

You do not have to exchange your time for money, so you can have more opportunities for other great things. You can explore other ways to improve your financial stability further.

You can also have time to research more about stocks, taxes, and investments. Thus, you can have better financial clarity and therefore propel you towards your financial objectives.

It is much easier to focus on finances when your mind is not occupied with a variety of things. Even though having problems is a natural part of life, you can have a better attitude towards dealing with them when you secure your finances.

For example, if something unpleasant and unexpected happens such as getting sick, getting into an accident, or getting robbed, you can recover faster if you have enough money and resources.

If you do not have the obligation to rush off to your job every single day, you may benefit from greater prosperity and growth over time. Whichever way you choose to view it, the importance of having a passive income is paramount.

In the next sections of this book, you will read about the different types of passive income streams that you can explore. Study them carefully and try them out to see if they are right for you.

1. RENT OUT SPACE VIA AIRBNB

AirBnB is a well-known online marketplace for homeowners and travelers alike. It is ideal for people who are willing to rent out their homes or a spare bedroom for a certain period of time.

AirBnB was founded in 2007 and has since become successful. It is the go-to place of travelers and vacationers who want to save money on lodging or accommodation.

How Does It Work?

To make money on AirBnB, you have to register your property and sign up as a host. Fill out the necessary forms and submit the required documents, such as descriptions and photos of your property.

Once your property is listed on the site, it will be viewed by travelers in search for accommodation in your area. These guests can look at the listings using different criteria such as price, destination, number of bedrooms, availability dates, facilities, amenities, and host language.

Prior to booking an accommodation via AirBnB, the guests can directly contact the host using the messaging service on the site. The official website of AirBnB is actually compatible with most computers and mobile devices.

For security purposes, the hosts have to provide the necessary identification. The travelers are also encouraged to posts reviews in order to build a good community. These reviews are not anonymous to establish trust.

With regard to payments and fees, you can rest assured that AirBnB has a secure platform. The payments are withheld until twenty-four hours after the guests arrive. There is also an available 24-hour hotline in case problems arise during the rental period.

As the host, you can set your price for accommodation, but AirBnB will charge you three percent of the payment transaction fee. If you want, you may also charge a cleaning fee and require a security deposit.

Legal Issues

Renting out some rooms or even your entire home to strangers for the weekend seems like a good idea for a passive income. However, before you begin this venture, see to it that you learn about all the legal aspects involved in it.

For starters, you have to find out if AirBnB is even legal in your area. Find out about your local laws and regulations. AirBnB is actually prohibited and subject to occupancy taxes in some places.

If AirBnB is legal in your area, you should still find out about any limitations. For instance, if you live in San Francisco, you only have a maximum of ninety days to be a host.

Is AirBnB Profitable?

Yes, it is. In fact, a lot of travelers prefer these rentals to hotels, hostels, and motels for a variety of reasons such as the following:

Cost

AirBnB rentals are usually cheaper than hotel rooms. Depending on your location, renting a whole house may actually be cheaper than a hotel suite.

Local Living

According to statistics, a lot of travelers want to feel as if they truly belong in the area where they are staying. They want to experience living locally. So, by renting a house, they are given the opportunity to explore the neighborhood and get in touch with those who live there.

Privacy

A lot of travelers want to have their own space. They want to feel at home even if they are far away from their real homes. Staying in a hotel and being surrounded by staff and other guests all the time will not give them the privacy that they want.

Peace and Quiet

Aside from privacy, travelers also want to have peace and quiet. They can book a home located in a quiet area rather than stay in a hotel with too many activities and too much noise coming from children, traffic, room service, etc.

See the Actual Premises

When you look up hotels on the Internet, you will see photos of identical rooms. These photos may even be touched up to look more attractive and bigger than they really are.

On the other hand, when you search for AirBnB rentals, you will see photos of real homes in real neighborhoods. You will see detailed descriptions of what you can expect to see once you get there.

Diversity

This is what attracts a lot of tourists and travelers alike. Unlike hotels, AirBnB is not limited to suites. Aside from regular houses, you can also choose from a variety of accommodations such as boathouses, light-houses, yachts, and even castles.

Kitchen

Most hotel rooms do not have a kitchen, and this is what turns off a lot of travelers. These people want to save money. So, they want to be able to prepare and cook their own food. With an AirBnB rental, they can do just that. Aside from saving money, they can ensure that their meals are clean, tasty, and nutritious.

More Space

Those who are travelling with family or friends would rather rent an entire house than individual hotel suites. This option is more cost-effective and practical. AirBnB makes it possible for a large group of people to stay together in one place without spending a lot of money.

How Can You Make Money via AirBnB?

In general, there are three ways on how you can make money on AirBnB.

First, you can rent out your own property. Since you own the place, you have full jurisdiction over it.

Secondly, you can rent out the place that you are renting. However, you need to ask permission from the owner first.

Lastly, you can manage a property that is being rented out to guests. You can work with landlords and receive payments or commissions for helping them rent out their property to travelers.

The Step-by-Step Process

Now that you have learned about the fundamentals of AirBnB rentals, including how they work and how you can make money from them, it is time to teach you the steps on how to actually engage in this business.

Step 1: Sign up

AirBnB listings are free of charge. You can create as many listings as you want. It is also easy to create these listings. Simply fill out the form with all the necessary information. Your listings would be kept private or hidden until you are ready to have them published.

You can also set a price for different rental duration. For instance, you can set daily, weekly, or monthly rates. You can even charge seasonal rates. This way, you can earn more money if there is a festival or sporting event in your town. You can also make a lot of money during the summer season especially if you live near the beach.

Step 2: Edit your page

Since you are the host, you can set your own house rules. Clearly define what you expect from your guests. Tell them what they are allowed and not allowed to do while on your property.

Use relevant descriptions and attractive photos to advertise your home. You may publish up to twenty-four photos on the site. Whenever a prospective guest becomes interested, he may contact you directly to ask questions.

As the host, you also have the right to accept and turn down booking requests. If you do not like a prospective guest for whatever reason, you are free to turn him down. Just make sure that you either accept or decline the offer in twenty-four hours.

The moment you accepted the reservation, you must coordinate a meeting schedule with the guest. Once his reservation has been completed, you may give a review or feedback. These reviews are great because they help build reference as well as establish a reputation for both the guest and the host.

Step 3: Consider a few crucial factors

See to it that you also consider certain factors before you rent out your property. For instance, you have to consider your location and amenities. If you are in a huge and busy city, you have a good chance of attracting lots of tourists, students on vacation, and businessmen.

New York, Paris, and Los Angeles are examples of cities frequented by tourists and travelers because of their beautiful museums, exciting night life, rich culture, delicious food, and nice tourist spots.

If you live near educational institutions, you can rent out your home to students. These young people want an inexpensive place to live and hang out. Just make sure that you get clear with the house rules so that your home will not be turned into a frat house.

Moreover, you can rent out your property to families or groups of friends who want to hold reunions and other events in your area. You can make a lot of money during peak seasons if you live near the mountains or oceans. These people most likely want to see a great view on their vacation.

You should also consider the amenities available. Is there a nearby bus stop if your home is quite far from the city? Is it possible to reach bookstores, restaurants, parks, and other tourist attractions by walking? Does your home have a parking lot, patio, or garden? Can your guests have their own private kitchen or bathroom if you are only renting out a room?

More importantly, you have to consider the safety and security of your guests as well as their belongings. Make sure that you also provide them with a hotline that they can contact in case of emergencies. For your own security, see to it that you also keep your belongings secured in a closet or room.

Step 4: Create listings

It is very easy to create a listing. In fact, you can finish one in just a couple of minutes. Simply follow the instructions shown on the website. Do not forget to incorporate the following essential elements in your listings to attract the attention of many guests:

a. Intriguing Headline

Nothing keeps a person's attention more than something they find intriguing. Choose a headline that is witty and interesting. It should capture the attention of the reader while giving him enough information at the same time.

Refrain from writing long narratives because they are boring. Keep your headlines brief but detailed. Sum up everything you want to convey in a single line. Remember that the headline is what people see first when they search for AirBnB rentals in your area. So, it has to be enticing.

b. Nice Profile

When you promote your home, you promote yourself as the host as well. Travelers usually go to AirBnB first whenever they want to search for inexpensive accommodations in a particular area. Likewise, they use the site to make immediate personal connections.

So, if you want to capture their attention, your profile should be warm and friendly. Upload a profile picture that makes you appear reliable and personable. Make sure that you also include relevant information to build trust. Your profile should make these prospective guests want to know you better.

c. Accurate Descriptions

It is important to be honest, detailed, and accurate when writing your descriptions about your property. Some people think that they have to exaggerate and make their homes seem better than they actually are to attract more guests. However, this strategy is not advisable and can backfire massively.

If you lie on your profile, you will be able to attract prospective guests immediately. However, once they find out the truth, they will leave negative reviews and feedback about you on AirBnB. The next time people check out your listings, they would find these bad reviews and get turned off right away.

Obviously, this is not good for your business. So, if you want to make AirBnB rentals work for you, you have to be honest. Do not make any claims or promises that you cannot deliver on as well. For example, if you said that guests can use your Wi-Fi connection, see to it that they actually can. Otherwise, they may file a complaint or even refuse to pay up.

You must also be upfront about what your guests can do on your property. Tell them what they can expect. For example, you can tell them if they can watch cable television, use Wi-Fi, use air conditioning or heater, take a hot shower, use the Jacuzzi or swimming pool, etc.

Tell them how many rooms are in your home and what type of beds you have. Families and groups of friends may prefer double deck beds while couples may prefer a queen sized bed where they can sleep together.

Make sure that you do not focus on the indoors alone. You must also disclose information about the surroundings. For example, you can reveal to your guests if you live on a busy street.

This way, people who do not want to hear traffic noises or be disturbed by yelling neighbors can avoid renting your home and getting disappointed. On the contrary, young people who prefer urban cities may like your property. They may enjoy its close proximity to bars, restaurants, coffee shops, and dance clubs.

d. Clear Photos

See to it that you take lots of clear photos of your property. Take a picture of every room and area, including your deck, balcony, or yard. This way, the guests can really have a feel of what your home is like.

Use a good camera to produce high quality photos. Take photos from different angles to really showcase your property. Use lighting fixtures if necessary to illuminate dark spots.

If you are not good at taking photos, you can use AirBnB's professional photography services. The company would send professional photographers over to your home to take pictures.

If you live in a good location, AirBnB may even let you avail of their professional photography services for free. You can take advantage of this perk if your photos can help increase the bookings made via AirBnB.

e. House Rules

You can choose from a wide variety of price structures and cancellation policies. You can also set your own house rules. For example, you can say that guests are not allowed to bring other people over or that they are not allowed to smoke.

Step 5: Determine the pricing and timing

Timing is one of the most important aspects of any business. Hence, you must always attempt to schedule an opening at the same time that a major event is happening in your area. This way, you can have more customers or clients.

Take the Super Bowl XLIX as an example. The AirBnB rentals in the Greater Phoenix area greatly profited from this sporting event. Because many people wanted to watch the game, they booked hotel rooms several months in advance. Those who were not prepared had no other choice but to turn to AirBnB rentals.

Last minute clients are actually willing to pay more money. They just want things to be taken care of in the soonest possible time, no matter how much money they have to pay for the services.

Do your best to get positive reviews. AirBnB gives a temporary boost to hosts. Take advantage of this good opportunity. In case your previous guest was not satisfied with his stay, you can still redeem yourself and overcome the negative review.

With regard to pricing, you can check out similar homes or properties to get an idea on how much you can rent out your home. Compare your listing with others so that you can set competitive prices.

If this is your first time to rent out your home, you may offer discounts. This way, you can attract more guests and encourage them to leave positive reviews. Most people like discounts and promos. You can even give your guests freebies or gifts to put them in a good mood.

Guests who were satisfied with your prices and services will most likely leave a positive feedback. So, offering discounted rates at first will not hurt your business. Once you have obtained enough positive reviews, you may raise your prices as well.

You can also find out if your rates are competitive enough by comparing them to the rates of nearby hotels. These places are usually expensive. Take Marriott, for instance. Its rates are at least $169 per night. Guests would have to pay more if they are inviting other people or having a party.

A good rule of thumb is to offer the same price as the hotels in your area. However, instead of merely renting out a room, you can rent out your entire home for this price. This would definitely make guests come to you.

Here are some more tips on how to determine the prices of your AirBnB rentals:

- Know how much your home is worth. What is its value? How much do you pay for mortgage or rent each month? Write down the price that you got and divide it by thirty. Once you get the answer, you can base your rate on this result.

- Study your competition. Observe what they do and how they conduct their business. Your competitors include hostels, hotels, campgrounds, and other Airbnb listings in your area. If you want guests to come to you instead of your competitors, you must be able to offer them better deals. For instance, you can offer a price within the same range as the other listings.

- Offer freebies, add-ons, and other perks. If your house has a washer and dryer, fancy linens, and cable, you can charge additional fees. You can also charge a higher rate than a nearby hotel if you offer a bottle of wine or a fruit basket to guests. You can also charge more if your guests have access to additional garage storage, communal space, or parking space.

- Set a high goal but start low. Since you are new in the industry, you have to set your priorities straight. Focus on attracting guests and obtaining positive reviews instead of beating your competitors. This could mean lowering your prices and giving freebies. Most travelers are in search of the least expensive accommodation. So if you see $100-listings, you may want to offer your place for only $75 per night to attract more views. Over time, you can increase your prices accordingly.

- Be aware of your limitations. AirBnB is basically an ecosystem that governs its own self. The prices of its services are dictated by the supply and demand. You can set your desired price range. However, in order for you to stay competitive on the market, you have to set your price close to what the other hosts offer. If your rate is too high, you will have a hard time attracting guests.

- Take holidays and special events into consideration. You may adjust your rates according to the significance of the event. For example, you can charge higher rates during the Christmas season or whenever there is a festival in your area. Hotels do this all the time. You can use the advanced pricing calendar and pricing tool of AirBnB to help you out.

- Factor in the security deposit. As much as possible, you should ask guests to give you a security deposit that is equivalent to a one night stay at your place. This is for your protection. In case something goes wrong, you can easily recover from the damages because you have funding. This security deposit can cover minor damages, such as scuffed flooring, broken appliances, and damaged furniture.

- Factor in the cleaning fee. Cleaning after guests is not easy, especially if they are a messy bunch. It takes a significant amount of money, energy, and time to complete this task. It does not really matter if you have a cleaning crew or maid to do this. You need to ask your guests to pay for the cleaning fee. This should cover the costs for cleaning bed sheets, mopping, vacuuming, and cleaning the rooms. How much you charge can depend on how big your house is.

- Charge additional fees for additional guests. It is common for guests to hold parties at the house they are staying in. After all, they are on a vacation and they want to have the time of their lives. To protect yourself, you should also charge extra for any additional person staying in your property.

- Charge lower fees for last minute bookings. You may consider dropping your prices if you have unoccupied dates coming up in the next few weeks. Rather than not make any money at all, it is much better to earn a profit from lower rates. You may even receive a positive feedback since guests generally want a good value for their money.

Step 6: Be a great host and earn positive feedback

Positive reviews can have a significant and long lasting impact on your reputation as a host. If you want prospective guests to see you as a credible and trustworthy person, you need to have good reviews that would prove your claims.

If your reviews are negative, guests may get turned off at first glance. This may persuade them to not do business with you even if you offer low rates and other perks.

Take note that your first few bookings are especially crucial because they set the tone for future bookings. Your first few reviews should be positive so you can attract more guests and have your listings on top of the search results.

How can you be a good host that gets positive reviews? Good communication is one requirement. You must connect and interact with your guests. Be cordial and friendly, too.

Communicate with them through different means, such as e-mail, text messages, and the Airbnb app. You should also be direct when telling them where to find your place, how they can park their cars and how they can get the keys to the house.

Whenever you receive inquiries or booking requests, you must be able to respond as soon as possible. You have to respond to them within a maximum of twenty-four hours.

Guests appreciate hosts who attend to them right away. The faster you reply to someone who inquires about your place, the more likely that person is going to make a booking. If you are not able to respond within a day, you can also get penalized by Airbnb.

You also have to keep your calendar updated. Even though the calendar automatically updates whenever a guest books a reservation, you still have to update your personal availability. Block the dates wherein you know you will not be available to host.

In addition, you have to make sure that your place is clean and orderly. Otherwise, your guests may not do repeat business with you in the future. Always have clean sheets, linens, and fixtures in the bedrooms.

Likewise, your bathroom and toilet should be clean. There should be no mildew or mold. Even your laundry area should be fresh. The same thing applies to the kitchen, living room, etc. Every room of your home should be welcoming to guests.

To make your guests even happier, you can offer little gifts such as a welcome basket filled with fruits, snacks, pastries, and local delicacies. You can also offer to personally pick them up from the airport, bus station, or train station. These perks and privileges can inspire them to give you positive reviews.

What are the Legal and Safety Issues Involved?

When Airbnb first started in 2012, there were hosts who had problems with guests. This is why the company re-evaluated their terms and conditions. Eventually, they offered a million-dollar guarantee to the hosts in order to cover the damages caused by guests.

There has been an instance wherein a host came home to find his property severely damaged. There was also a host who found meth pipes left in his home. Then, there was this host who was locked out from his own home by guests who refuse to leave.

Naturally, you want your AirBnB business to succeed. Then again, you must never compromise your safety and security. Keep in mind that you are not obligated to say yes to every reservation request. You are free to check out and evaluate guest profiles.

Do not hesitate to trust your instinct and turn out prospective guests that you do not like. While declining these people may affect your host metrics, it is a small price to pay for your safety and security. Your mental health is very important, too. When you do not encounter problematic guests, you can have less stress.

Anyway, AirBnB has also been subject to legal issues with regard to hotel taxes. It has also encountered issues that involved hosts renting out properties that are not zoned out for rentals. Likewise, there have been incidents in which renters have violated the lease policies and sublet their apartment or condo units.

The truth is that a lot of individuals rent out their homes on AirBnB in spite of lease restrictions or improper zoning issues. These actions are very risky. If you do not want to have any problems, make sure that you always abide by the laws in your state.

AirBnB may be lucrative, but it is not for everyone. Carefully assess yourself and your condition before you choose this kind of business.

How to Prevent Damage to Property

One of the main concerns of individuals who rent out their space to guests is that their property might get trashed or damaged. As a host, it is only natural for you to think about the condition of your personal belongings when you are away and other people are in your home.

You may wonder if your guests are unsanitary or reckless. You may worry that they would steal or contaminate your stuff. Your concerns are reasonable and understandable.

Fortunately, AirBnB has already foreseen this. They are prepared to deal with such situations. Hence, they have come up with protective measures to help guarantee your safety and security.

The Host Guarantee

Airbnb offers a $1,000,000 insurance policy to hosts. They would receive the money if their property gets severely damaged. However, this insurance policy does not cover personal liability, normal wear and tear, pet damage, and stolen or damaged cash, securities, rare artwork, collectibles, and jewelry.

Risks Involved with AirBnB Hosting

Aside from the possibility of your property being trashed or damaged, you also put your personal safety at risk when you rent out your home to strangers. Unlawful individuals do not only steal money and things. They also tend to steal identities.

Thus, you need to make sure that you keep your personal documents in a secure location. Birth certificate copies, identification cards, passport, driver's license, and other things that contain your personal and financial information should be kept away from your guests.

If you do not protect yourself, your identity can be used to commit fraud. The thieves can even steal your medical insurance data and consequently put your health at risk.

How Can You Protect Yourself?

Even though hosting on AirBnB is pretty much hassle free, you should still follow these tips for your own protection:

1. Review the profiles of prospective guests

AirBnB is a public network. It is open to everyone just like any other social networks. The hosts and the guests have to upload profiles that include their personal details, pictures, videos, references, and reviews.

A good rule of thumb is to review the profiles of prospective guests before accepting their reservation requests. Make sure that you also contain their personal references and read their reviews to have an idea of what they are like.

2. Add a security deposit to your listing

Hosts are not required to ask for security deposits. However, you should not be too optimistic. Preparing yourself for possible unpleasant results can help save you. Make it a habit to always ask for a security deposit beforehand.

You can charge between $100 and $5000. This amount should be able to cover the basics. Your guests have to give their security deposit before they make a reservation.

In case a problem arises during the rental period, you should report it within forty-eight hours. Otherwise, you would have to give back the security deposit.

3. Send a message to prospective guests before accepting their reservations

Start a conversation with individuals who express a desire to book your place. Get to know them better and establish rapport. Ask them why they are in town, how long they are staying, what they do for a living, or how many people they are traveling with. Chatting up prospective guests lets you gain more vital information about them.

4. Have reservation requirements

AirBnB deals with application approval. Nevertheless, you can still ask prospective guests to show proof of identity. For instance, you can ask them to present at least one government issued ID or any other valid ID.

5. Establish clear guidelines

Clearly define what you want to happen when you accept the reservation requests of prospective guests. As a host, you are allowed to have your own House Manual and House Rules.

Your House Manual can contain private information that is only accessible by approved guests. You can include your Wi-Fi password, instructions on how to use your appliances, and other helpful information such as where they can find the nearest bus station or restaurants.

Your House Rules should clearly state what your guests can and cannot do in your home during their stay. You can make these rules accessible by prospective guests so that they would know what they are going for.

6. Get off-site protected storage.

Safety deposit boxes can significantly improve your AirBnB hosting experience. You can use them to store your jewelry, cash, and valuable documents. Local banks typically offer them for free or for a small fee.

If you have delicate artwork, firearms, collectibles, or furs, you can store them in a climate-controlled storage space to preserve their quality.

7. Do a due diligence on guests.

If you want to qualify for the Host Guarantee offered by AirBnB, you need to do a due diligence on your guests. Evaluate their profiles carefully and do a background check. Use all the available sources that you can find, including Google, Facebook, LinkedIn, etc. Find out as much information as possible.

8. Get a P.O. Box for your mail or stop it temporarily.

No matter how many times you check out your guests' profiles, you still cannot be sure about their behaviors. They might have this habit of reading other people's letters.

So, in order to protect your personal mail while you are away, you should get a P.O. box. You can also ask your local post office to keep your mail on hold temporarily.

9. Automate the syncing process using electronic devices

You can use your computer, tablet, or mobile device to make sure that every transaction goes smoothly. Having a digital copy aside from a physical copy ensures that your data remains consistent and safe. Do not forget to have a master sheet. It must be a physical copy of your bookings or reservations.

10. Automate the syncing process using software programs

If you do not want to input booking or reservation information manually, you can use a software program. For example, you can use Guesty and Pillow.

With Guesty, you can outsource guest communications for twenty-four hours. It will help you stay on top of every booking and reservation. Even when you are away or sleeping, it will approve your guests based on your pre-arranged profile.

Likewise, Pillow will automate your listings across a variety of platforms. You can make a listing of your property and have it uploaded on numerous rental sites. You can also benefit from full property management in different areas.

What Are the Protocols On Cleaning?

It is typical for guests to not clean up after themselves when staying in hotels, motels, hostels, and AirBnB rentals. So, in order to save yourself the trouble, you should charge for cleaning services.

You can either clean your property yourself or hire professionals to do the job. Either way, the cleaning fees you charge should be enough to pay the people you hire or to compensate you for your time and effort.

When setting a rate, you can base it on the size of your property. For example, you can charge $50 for a medium-sized house. You can charge a higher fee if your house is bigger. The cleaning fee should cover the costs of washing the sheets, mopping the floors, vacuuming the carpets, and cleaning the rooms.

Getting professionals to clean your property for you is not a problem. If you live in New York, you can use Get Maid. If you live in Los Angeles, you can use Hostwise. If you need someone to clean your place as soon as possible, you can use Handy.

These people have been cleaning homes and other establishments for years. They know what they are doing. So, unless you are an expert at cleaning yourself, you better leave the cleaning job to the professionals. If you insist on doing the task yourself, you might risk damaging your furniture or carpets further.

When it comes to choosing a cleaning service, see to it that you factor in reliability and flexibility of schedule. If you choose to go with a major company, you can benefit from expense tracking and easy to use reporting. However, they also tend to charge a high rate for their services.

You can ask the cleaning staff to send you a before and after photo of the area. This way, you can see the state in which your guests left your property. You should also tell the cleaning staff how you want the house to be cleaned.

For example, you can request for certain types of detergents to be avoided if you have delicate carpets or flooring. You can recommend your preferred cleaning solution.

You can also give instructions as to what room you want to be cleaned first,. If you want your carpets, sofas, and other belongings cleaned in a particular way, you should tell the cleaning staff about it too.

How Can You Take Care of Your Guests?

Your guests will be inclined to do repeat business with you if you show them hospitality and genuine care. So, throughout the duration of their stay on your property, you should check on them frequently to ensure that they have everything they need. Ask them how they are and if they need any assistance.

Communicate with your guests on a regular basis. Just know when you talk too little or too much. You may even offer to give them a tour of your area or to give them directions towards the best tourist spots and dining places.

Your guests would surely appreciate the time and effort that you exert to make them feel special. In addition, you should make sure that your guests are safe and secure. Give them instructions on how to contact the nearest police, fire department, or hospital in case of emergency.

AirBnB is very popular across the globe. You literally have thousands of competitors. So, you need to stand out and make people know how great of a host you are. Give your guests an experience they will always remember. So, the next time they visit your city, they would not hesitate to book your place again.

Even better, these satisfied guests will recommend you to their family and friends. They will also give you glowing reviews; thus, increasing your credibility and trustworthiness further.

If they have blogs, websites, or social media accounts, it is also likely that they would talk about you and their wonderful experience in your home. They would upload photos and videos, thereby increasing your popularity. Going the extra mile for your guests will surely pay off in the long run.

How Can You Follow Up On Your Guests?

Since you know how many days or weeks your guests are staying on your property, you can prepare for the exit and follow up process ahead of time. See to it that you double check with your guests before they close the reservation. Send them boilerplate e-mails, automated messages, and reminders for checkout.

You can send your guests a text message or e-mail after their stay on your property. You can ask them what they thought of their stay and how they felt. Encourage them to leave you a feedback. You can also send a thank you note with flowers or tokens.

How Can You Manage Your Finances Effectively?

AirBnB is a pretty lucrative business. No wonder more and more homeowners are being enticed to rent out there homes. If you have more than one house, apartment, or condo unit that you list on AirBnB, make sure that you have a separate bank account for each and every one of them. This way, you can sort out your finances better and avoid confusion when you do your inventory.

Likewise, make sure that you have separate records for utility payments, cleaning fees, and other expenses. You need to have a physical and digital copy of your computations. You can store the physical copies in your file cabinet and keep the digital copies in your electronic devices. In case your physical files get lost, stolen, or damaged, you can use your digital files. Conversely, you can rely on your physical copies in case your digital files are deleted or lost.

It is also good practice to invest at least ten percent of your profits into home maintenance. This is especially true if you rely on AirBnB to sustain your personal expenses. You need to keep your property in top condition. Prospective guests would not be attracted to your home if it is not well maintained.

In addition, lack of maintenance can cause your house to deteriorate; thus, reducing its aesthetics and functionality. This can lower its value in case you decide to sell it on the housing market. You may also incur more expenses when you finally decide to have it repaired. Keep in mind that it is always better to prevent damage than to fix it.

The rest of your profits should go to your savings. You may also invest in more properties to further expand your business. Then again, you need to gain enough experience first. This way, you will not have a hard time trying to manage multiple homes and units all at once. You will also be exposed to connections who can help you grow your business.

Do your best to retain a good standing on AirBnB so that you can have a steady cash flow. As you know, businesses generally survive on cash flow. This is why you must always be liquid. If you do not make enough money, you will not be able to pay for succeeding reservations.

How Can You Resolve Disputes?

No business opportunity is perfect. As the saying goes, if it is too good to be true, then it probably is. AirBnB has had its shares of disputes and legal issues. Nevertheless, it has always managed to come through.

At present, AirBnB has an insurance policy for hosts to protect their property against damages. This Host Guarantee can help you avoid incurring unnecessary expenses. Then again, you should not rely on it alone. You also have to be wise as a host.

Familiarize yourself with the rules of the platform. This way, you can resolve any dispute on your own with ease. If necessary, you may seek help from a legal team. You are allowed to set your own house rules. So, make sure that you use that to your advantage.

A good rule of thumb is to go with the tightest policy to make sure that you do not end up on the losing end. Tight policies would protect you against guest who do not follow the rules, misbehave, and abuse their freedom.

You may also want to install CCTV cameras all over your property. This way, you can easily monitor the activities of your guests. It would let you know if they damage certain furniture or appliances, as well as give you proof of their misbehavior.

Just make sure to avoid invading their privacy. While it is a good idea to install CCTV cameras in common areas such as the living room, kitchen, and patio, you should avoid installing them in the bedroom and bathroom.

AirBnB also requires hosts to disclose any surveillance devices or security CCTV cameras in their listings. They should also inform the guests if an active recording is occurring.

Aside from the CCTV footage, you can also use photos as evidences. For example, if your guests trashed your home, you can use the photos taken by the cleaning staff you hired to clean up the place.

Having sufficient evidence will let you resolve disputes much faster and more efficiently. You will also have a basis on how much to charge your guests for damages.

With regard to proof of communication, you can use the text messages and e-mails that you sent to and received from your guests. You can also use any recorded phone messages.

Hopefully, you should be able to settle disputes without having to file legal charges or go to court.

How Can You Manage Your Social Relations?

Some people purchase apartments and condominium units specifically to serve as AirBnB rentals. These people are immersed in the business. They do not personally live in the units that they lease.

So, what about those who rent out their actual living spaces? If you are one of these people, you need to make sure that you maintain good social relations with everyone. Otherwise, you will have a hard time getting guests as well as be in bad blood with your neighbors.

You need to select your guests carefully if they are about to live in your neighborhood for a while. Consider how your neighbors might feel about you renting out your place to college students, foreign tourists, groups of bachelorettes, etc. The way they behave during their stay on your property can either reflect positively or negatively on you.

State it clearly in your house rules that your guests are not allowed to play loud music or to have parties late at night if you live in a quiet suburb. You can also make it up to your neighbors by referring their business to your guests. For example, you can recommend their coffee shop, bakery, or diner.

What Should You Remember With Regard to Reviews?

Guest or client reviews are great because they help establish reputation and build up reference. They also determine the validity of the guest and the host. Prospective guests can look at these reviews to help them decide if they want to rent the place or not.

As the host, you can write reviews about your guests too. Make sure that you are honest and unbiased with your reviews. Most hosts give positive feedback to guests who give them positive feedback as well. Likewise, they tend to skip giving any feedback to unsatisfied guests who might give them a negative review.

What if you get a negative review? Is this the end of your career as an AirBnB host? Do not fret just yet. If you ever receive a negative review, you can always give an explanation for it. In cases of retaliation reviews, see to it that you clarify your points and explain your situation well.

Do not be afraid to tell your side of the story so that people can know your version of the truth. Then again, you should not get too carried away with the negative feedback on your profile. You can still have a successful AirBnB rental business if you have more positive reviews than negative ones.

In addition, keep in mind that it is actually much better to see any kind of feedback on a profile than none at all. Lack of information can make space for suspicions and rumors. This can hurt your business even worse.

Too much information, on the other hand, can be a pleasant surprise. It can work in your favor by shifting the focus of contention and making prospective guests think that your negative feedback is not really a true reflection of you as a host.

Is Your Emotional Energy Important?

Yes, it is. Your emotional wellness is just as important as your physical and mental health. You need to take good care of yourself so that you do not get burned out.

Take breaks whenever you have to. If you feel that hosting is being too stressful, you can take a step back. Otherwise, you might get sick and no longer be able to do your duties as a host.

You should also learn how to delegate certain tasks. Do not be afraid to ask for help or to reach out to someone if you feel that hosting is giving you anxiety. AirBnB is a great way to earn a passive income. However, if it is too much for you to deal with, then you may want to consider shifting to other passive income streams.

2. PLACE ADS ON YOUR CAR, SHOP, ETC.

If you have a car and you travel frequently, you can wrap ads on your vehicle for some extra money. Car vinyl display advertisements are actually very popular today.

Likewise, you can place ad stickers on your store windows. A lot of brands are actually willing to pay people to help advertise their business via ad stickers.

Placing Ads on Your Car

What is Car Wrapping?

This money making opportunity involves the use of cars and other vehicles for advertising products and/or services. Decal stickers are either fully wrapped around the car or simply placed on its sides. Their main purpose is to get the message of advertisers out to the public.

More often than not, those who choose to make money through this method are required to drive to specific places in order to target the right audience. For example, plumbing services may be advertised to homeowners in suburbs.

People tend to pay more attention to moving objects on the road. Hence, ads on moving cars are more effective than static ads on billboards. If you show them a completely wrapped vehicle, this vehicle would stand out from the rest.

If done properly, car vinyl display advertisements can be ninety-six percent more effective than billboards.

What Types of Ads Can Be Placed on Cars?

The ads may differ from one company to another. Small business owners, for example, may want to market their products locally. Major corporations may also use these ads to gain more traction for their brand.

The vinyl stickers placed on cars typically show the company trademark or logo. The more ads there are, the more money you can earn. So, if you want to maximize your earning potential, you should have your entire vehicle covered with ads. You can make more money if your vehicle is huge.

Are You Qualified for this Money Making Opportunity?

Sadly, not all car owners and drivers are qualified to earn money by placing ads on their vehicles. You have to undergo a screening process before your application can be approved.

For starters, you will be asked about the year as well as the make and model of your car. You will also be asked about the usual route that you take and the number of hours that you spend on the road.

Companies want their ads to be seen by as many people as possible. They also want to ensure that their ads are spread equally and placed accordingly. So, if you do not get out there often or if you do not drive in a busy street, your application may be rejected.

There is also usually a required mileage. You have to maintain at least the minimum mileage every week. If you are a cab driver, this money making opportunity may work well for you.

See to it that you follow the rules of the company. Be aware of the possible restrictions and limitations, such as not being allowed to use personal bumper stickers.

Once you are deemed qualified to earn money by placing ads on your car, you have to wait for the company to contact you. You will discuss the types of ads you have to use as well as how much money you will earn.

On average, drivers earn $400 each month through car vinyl display ads. Nonetheless, you can earn more money depending on your driving routine, type of vehicle, and time spent on the road.

In essence, you should be of legal age to drive. You should also have a good driving record. See to it that your ads are on their proper spots throughout the duration of your contact.

You should also meet the minimum monthly requirement for mileage as well as have a GPS installed in your vehicle. This GPS may either come from the company or from you.

What If You Do Not Own a Car?

Is it possible to benefit from this money making opportunity if you do not own a car? The answer is yes.

Some companies do not require drivers to have their own cars. This is what is referred to as 'free car promotion'. The company would be the one to provide the car with the stickers or decals. It is already pre-wrapped with the ads. So, all you have to do is get inside and drive it around.

Then again, this setup usually comes with a specific set of terms and conditions that you need to follow.

Placing Ads on Your Shop

Cars are not the only places where ad stickers are ideal to be placed. You can also put stickers all around your shop, such as on your windows, doors, walls, and even floors.

Stickers are an effective yet inexpensive way to promote business. They are used by both small business owners who are just starting out and major companies that have been in the industry for decades.

Can You Profit from Placing Ad Stickers on Your Shop?

Yes, you can. This is especially true if the sticker has a nice design that appeals to the company's customer base. You can contact companies and ask them if they are willing to partner with you. You can help promote their business in exchange for a fee or commission.

A lot of companies whose sole form of advertisement is stickers have had an increase in sales by as much as 550%. This is not really surprising because stickers can be customized easily. Business owners can be as creative as they want to be. For instance, the Apple Store has a broken glass sticker on its window. It uses this sticker to endorse the iPod Hi-Fi.

However, you should not limit yourself to just the big name companies. You can also go to local businesses and ask if you can add their stickers to your store window and countertop. In return, they can pay you or place your own business stickers in their headquarters. This would expose you to more prospective clients.

You have a better chance of being selected by companies if your shop is located in a busy area. The more people go to your shop, the more exposure these ad stickers will get.

What are the Possible Drawbacks?

You have to consider the ordinances in your city. There might be rules against posting materials, such as stickers on municipal property, for example. You should also make sure that you do not post stickers in possibly nuisance locations to avoid getting negative feedback.

Where Else Can You Place Ad Stickers?

As you know, stickers are versatile marketing tools that can open up more possibilities for promotions. Aside from vehicles and shops, you can also use them on product packaging and place in various places all over your community.

At times, the product packaging becomes the deciding factor as to whether customers will buy the products or not. Hence, you should place your stickers strategically.

For instance, you should put emphasis on vital sales information. You can include ingredients, features, or instructions on how to use the product.

You can also place ad stickers on posts, poles, bench armrests, and signs. Just make sure that you ask permission first in order to avoid facing legal issues. Do not place your stickers on restricted areas.

3. FRANCHISE A BUSINESS

Starting a business from scratch is time-consuming, challenging, and involves a lot of hard work. It is not for everyone. Fortunately, you can still run a business by buying a franchise. Having an already existing business model can help you make good profits.

What Exactly Is a Franchise?

Simply put, investing in a business franchise is a licensing relationship. Companies, such as 7-Eleven and Subway, license their brands, operating systems, and products to whoever acquires a franchise. This is what you call 'business format franchising'.

Some examples of franchises include fast food chains, restaurants, home cleaning, child learning centers, medical clinics, tax preparation, UPS stores, car repair shops, and flower shops.

Just like most businesses, franchises involve upfront funding. You have to pay for the franchise fee, which is significantly variable. For example, the start-up fees associated with a McDonald's franchise is typically around $1,000,000 to $2,300,000 while the start-up fees associated with a Subway franchise is usually around $116,000 to $263,000 only.

A McDonald's franchise costs more money than a Subway franchise because it is bigger, more popular, and offers more products. Whichever business franchise you choose, you would be establishing a relationship with the company that gives you the right to advertise and sell using their products and trademarks. Of course, you have to follow the rules and pay the fees involved.

What are the Pros and Cons of Franchising a Business?

Before you shell out money for a franchise, it would be in your best interest to learn about the pros and cons associated with this money making opportunity first.

The Pros:

Tried and Tested Business Model

There is no need for you to start from scratch and figure things out. Everything has already been done, including research and development. You have an existing and successful business process right in front of you. So, you can easily earn a profit.

Brand Name Recognition

Promoting and marketing the franchise will not be a problem since it has already established a reputation for itself. People are familiar with the business, and they trust it. So, you do not have to exert a lot of effort in convincing customers and clients to do business with you.

Support and Training

Franchisers typically provide training to their franchisees. You will be taught about the business model as well as given helpful advice on how to run a successful business.

The Cons

Initial Funding

At times, the initial capital necessary for a franchise is even larger than the amount you need to start a business from scratch. Certain franchises require more money than others. So, if you really want a specific franchise, you have to have the money to buy it.

Lack of Flexibility

Since you are not the one who started the business, you do not have full control over it. You cannot simply make a modification in the business model. Otherwise, the reputation of the company will be at stake. In general, you have to do most of the things that the franchiser or company wants.

Continuous Royalty Fees

Franchisers usually require ongoing payments or a percentage of the gross sales. This is how major corporations make money.

Time-Consuming

When you operate a franchise, you run a business. This means that you have to spend enough time to make sure that everything is under control. Even though you have a tried and tested business model, you cannot simply leave the franchise on its own. You need to have a good management of the business. Give it enough time, effort, and energy.

Comes with Risks

Just like any other business, franchises come with risks. For instance, even though you have a reliable business model and a popular brand name, you still cannot be sure that you will earn a lot of money. If your location is not good, you may not get a lot of customers.

How Much Money Should You Prepare for a Franchise?

With regard to costs, the initial franchise is merely the starting point. You have to consider the other factors involved with running this business.

For instance, aside from the initial franchise fee, you also have to pay for the expenses associated with training and rent. Another consideration is on paint and tenant improvements as well as equipment, supplies, signs, and furniture.

You also have to spend on annual insurance, business name registration, and business licenses. To ensure that your business is protected and running smoothly, you would need to allot a budget for professional services such as accounting and legal fees.

There are also bills for utility and phone. Plus, you need to shell out money for video surveillance and other related equipment. Lastly, you will spend on pre-opening ads to inform people about your business as well as additional reserve funding.

Buying a franchise can really be a handful. You need to be financially prepared for the initial fee and other costs involved. Do not worry though, there is a huge likelihood that the money you spend at the beginning would have great payoffs in the long run.

Is a Franchise an Ideal Passive Income Source?

Yes, it is. However, you need to consider all the factors involved in order to succeed in this venture. For instance, you have to consider your funding and location. If you do not have enough money on your bank account, you can obtain a business loan. Choose a spot that is frequented by your target customers.

In addition, you have to pass the screening process of the franchiser or company. These entities are often in search of partners who have a huge likelihood for being successful and making their brand even more successful.

How to Choose the Right Business Franchise

Before you go after any business franchise, you have to know your true self. You have to be really honest about what you want to achieve and how capable you are to run this kind of business.

For starters, you have to answer the following questions with complete honesty to determine which franchise is suitable for you:

1. What do you aim to get from a business franchise?

People go after business franchise opportunities for different reasons. Some of them go for it because they are passionate about it and they see it as a profitable hobby. These people still continue to work on their day jobs.

Others, however, go for it because they want it to be their main income source. There are also those who want to build equity as well as those who aim to have more than one business franchise.

Jeff Elgin, the CEO of Minnesota-based franchise consulting firm FranChoice, said that the type of business you choose actually stems from what you want to accomplish.

2. What are your personal goals?

Every person has his own motivations and objectives for wanting to become a businessman.

Ask yourself about your personal goals. Why do you want to start a business? Do you want to make a lot of money? Do you want to have more free time at home? Do you want to advance your career through this entrepreneurial step?

Once you figure out what your real goals are, you will be able to identify which business franchise is an ideal fit for you to be able to meet these goals.

3. How much money should you invest or are willing to invest?

It is important to have a realistic sense of what business opportunities you can have with your available budget. Just like any other business ventures, you should not expect to earn lots of profits right away. Hence, you need to have enough money for your needs as you get off the ground.

The costs of franchise businesses generally vary, depending on what business model they have and what industry they are in. Terry Powell is the CEO and founder of The Entrepreneur's Source, which is a franchise business coaching company.

According to him, franchise businesses typically require upfront fees that range from $10,000 to $1 million. Those who want to have a franchise must weigh their initial investments against their expected returns. They must also consider their equity goals, wealth, income, and lifestyle.

Also, you have to remember that loans are not always easy to obtain. You need to have at least $200,000 to cover your working capital, franchise fee, equipment, and inventory among other expenses if you do not have a physical location.

If this is the case, you may find it difficult to get a loan from banks. You need to have more than $200,000 plus a good credit standing in order for you to be approved for loans.

You can search the Internet for inexpensive franchise opportunities.

Just make sure that you are very careful. Cheap businesses tend to have high turnover rates. They also tend to be more competitive and saturated. They may not even provide sufficient training and support. Even worse, you may not be able to resell them. Thus, they can end up being more expensive than other franchise opportunities.

4. What is your exit strategy?

Unfortunately, a lot of prospective franchisees neglect this question. They are so focused on getting started that they forget to think of how they would get out of the business.

It is important for you to be honest to yourself with regard to how long you think you can stay in the business. Do you plan to only be in the business for a certain number of years or do you want to run it for the rest of your life?

Your answer to this question is very important because franchisers tend to have varying restrictions with regard to selling to other franchisers. There are franchise businesses that are not even scaleable to begin with.

5. How much risk can you take?

Go through your financials thoroughly. Review every detail so that you can get a sense of how much risk you can take. Then again, see to it that you also take your personality into consideration. What is your risk-averse level?

According to Mark Siebert, CEO of Illinois-based franchise consulting group iFranchise, there are plenty of companies that have long franchising success records yet they are no longer on the cutting edge. On the other hand, there are newer companies that are riskier yet have a better chance of producing higher returns.

6. How much involvement do you want to have in the business?

You need to determine the role that you wish to play in the business early on. Some franchisees prefer to have a direct involvement in the delivery of products or services.

Others, however, choose to become absentee owners because they have a full time day job. These owners do not directly run the business. Instead, they hire people to manage and operate it on a daily basis.

You have to figure out what you want to do. Do you want to work on a specific task every single day? Do you prefer to lead a company? Do you prefer to manage managers?

Think of how many days you can work. For instance, if you can only work at daytime during weekdays, you lose two-thirds of the available franchise business opportunities.

7. What are your strengths?

Basically, you have to come up with a list of the things that you are good at. Evaluate your skill set and experiences. What have you learned from previous business ventures and professional experiences?

Determine which area you are comfortable as well. For example, are you comfortable with cold calling or sales? Do you enjoy interacting with clients behind the counter? Do you have the skills to manage people? Do you enjoy field work with customers?

Identify the tasks that you can do yourself and the ones that you can delegate to other people. For example, if you do not have an accounting or bookkeeping background, you can hire someone else to deal with that part of the business. You can hire an accountant or outsource to a company that specializes in this area.

It is okay if you are not yet an expert in a particular field, as long as you possess the necessary skills. You can learn and improve along the way. This is what is great about franchising. You can totally reinvent yourself and move into an entirely new industry. You can leave the expertise to the franchiser himself.

8. How important is status for you?

How much do you value the opinion of other people? Say, a friend or acquaintance asks you what you do for a living. Will you be comfortable admitting that you run a business of scrubbing grease off fast food kitchen hoods?

If you are too concerned about social status, you might find it embarrassing to discuss the nature of your business with other people, especially at parties and events.

However, if you are a more practical person, you would be more concerned about competition. More often than not, these seemingly unattractive or disgusting business ventures produce a lot of money because they do not have a lot of competition.

What Should You Ask the Franchiser?

Now that you have gotten more acquainted with yourself, you have to get more acquainted with the franchiser.

According to Alan George, Franchise Marketing Systems vice president, you have to ask the parent company questions that may or may not be tackled in the franchise disclosure document. For example, you can ask about the sales approach.

You can also ask if there is enough available business on the market as well as if you have sufficient funding for campaigns. Do not forget to ask about the advertising and sales approaches, including whether or not they may work in the market.

Furthermore, WineStyles Tasting Station CEO Bryan McGinness said that prospective franchisees have to be clear on what franchisers expect of them and vice versa. This way, both parties can have a long lasting business relationship.

What Should You Look for In a Business Franchise Opportunity?

Once you have identified the business model and field that you prefer, you should study the attributes of companies. The following are some of the attributes that you should see:

- Strong support system

  You are buying into a business with a tried and tested business model. Hence, it is only fitting that you receive a good amount of support through every stage of the way. You should be able to get in touch with people who can guide and help you.

- Investment in potential

  The franchiser or company should genuinely care about their franchisees. They should not only focus on earning money, but they should aim to help you reach your maximum potential as well. Both of you should determine early on if you are business-minded and have a desire to grow with the company.

The Franchise Disclosure Document (FDD) Review

Michael Daigle is a partner at Cheng Cohen, which is a franchise industry law firm. According to him, you need to have a legal adviser or a financial adviser who can help you read and understand the franchise disclosure document.

The following are some of the sections that you have to pay attention to:

Past or Current Litigation

You will read about the experience of the franchiser as well as whether or not the franchiser and his team has been involved in litigation or bankruptcies that are relevant to their experiences as a franchiser or to the brand.

The historical and existing litigation between the franchiser and the franchisee may show some dissatisfaction with the system. It may also show that the franchiser seriously wants to uphold his system standards so that all franchisees can benefit from them.

Revenue Model and Payments

You will also read about what you have to pay to the franchiser and his affiliates before and after the opening of the business. In addition, you will learn how much the franchiser depends on his franchisees for profit. You should be able to see the financial standing of the units.

Turnover and Resource Strain

You will see a list of franchisees who are still in the system as well as those who have already exited. It is strongly encouraged that you contact these franchisees so that you can learn about their profitability, experiences, and struggles.

Do not hesitate to ask questions. In fact, you should ask similar questions to different franchisees. This way, you can compare their answers. Make sure that you examine both positive and negative feedbacks without bias.

4. RENT OUT YOUR TOOLS

Another ideal way on how to generate a passive income is by investing in expensive equipment and tools and then renting them out. Your clients will be individuals who only need such equipment and tools occasionally. Rather than shell out a huge amount of money for something that they will not use on a regular basis, they would choose to rent.

Renting out equipment and tools can be a lucrative venture. Equipment owners can even earn a steady income stream. Moreover, those who work in an industry in which specialized equipment and tools are necessary can earn money from their current assets, too.

The Pros of Renting Out Equipment and Tools

If you do not frequently use your equipment and tools, renting them out would ensure that they do not corrode. Regular use can save them from being destroyed by rust and extend their lifetime.

In addition, renting out your things can give you a much better return if they are in use and giving you income. These tools do not generate any revenue when they are merely kept in their storage units.

There is no need for you to shell out more money when you rent out your tools. You also do not have to worry about your credit to debit ratio being affected. In fact, you may use the profits to invest in more equipment and tools that you can rent out.

You may also sign a contract with a rental company and have them manage the rental process for you. They would be the ones responsible for maintaining your equipment, so you can sit back and relax. They would also be the ones to provide the insurance in case the tools get damaged. Just take note of the fees involved with hiring a rental company.

Practical Tips on How to Start an Equipment and Tool Rental Business

Before you start any business, see to it that you study all aspects carefully. Learn from the mistakes and success stories of people who have taken the same path as yours and achieved success. Here are some tips that you may find useful:

Study the market continuously

You should never stop studying the market. Trends come and go all the time, and you have to stay updated. Try to provide the tools that customers or clients actually need.

In order to gain reliable statistics, you could conduct a survey in your area. Ask the residents about the equipment and tools that they need the most. Do not make the mistake of having idle inventory. This can end your business, especially if you have to make a lot of payments for the equipment. See to it that you choose the right tools to invest in.

If you choose not to work with a rental company, see to it that you set realistic and affordable rates to make a good profit. Use the Internet to establish an online presence. Take advantage of social media platforms to reach a wider set of audience.

Be responsive to the queries of customers and try to build rapport. Engage with them by having short conversations and encouraging them to share your posts. Make sure that you also post pictures of your equipment and tools so that people can see how they look like.

Treat your customers or clients properly so they would be encouraged to do repeat business with you. Set up a hassle-free environment for them and do not over negotiate.

In addition, you have to be willing to accept some of the terms of your customers as you sign an agreement. This would show that you truly value them in your business.

Of course, you have to maintain your equipment and tools regularly. After all, your entire business depends on working equipment. See to it that they are in good shape. Do not delay anything that has to be fixed or dealt with right away.

Recommended Rental Equipment to Invest In

The following are some of the most commonly used equipment and tools. It is advisable that you invest in them to earn a good profit.

Aerial Lift

This equipment may be invaluable to your business. It can be used for a lot of things, such as painting, landscaping, and construction. It will surely be high in demand.

Forklift

Its use typically ranges from industry warehouses to huge department stores. It is a powered industrial truck that moves material over short distances. As much as possible, you should get forklifts in different capacities and sizes to meet the needs of your clients.

Landscape Equipment

Companies often need additional landscape equipment for their projects. Even homeowners sometimes need this equipment for lawn and garden maintenance.

Offering a full-service equipment fleet may prove to be lucrative if you have specialized equipment. You can invest in straw blowers, tillers, mortar mixers, landscaping tractors, paver saws, two-man augers, trenchers, and light compaction equipment.

Excavator

You must consider the terrain and the nature of the project when you get an excavator. Nonetheless, you can invest in a crawler excavator, caterpillar hydraulic excavator, suction excavators, and backhoe.

Track Loader

This equipment is indispensable whether you are constructing a small foundation or a home project. It is a versatile earthmover that can move in small areas as well as work in construction sites.

Common Mistakes and Pitfalls

The following are some of the most common mistakes and pitfalls that people make when renting out their equipment and tools. Make sure that you learn from them so that you can minimize your errors and maximize your gains.

Not Disclosing Conditions for Added Costs for Damage or Usage in the Rental Contract

It is always best to be honest and upfront about anything with regard to your business. If you have any additional fees, you have to inform your clients so that they would be adequately prepared. Surprising them will only turn them off and prevent them from doing any more business with you in the future.

Not Setting Realistic Rates or Setting Very Low Rates for Costly Equipment during the Beginning of the Business

This is a common mistake among new business owners. They want to attract the attention of prospective clients, so they offer their rental equipment and tools for very low rates even though they bought them at such high prices. If you do not become realistic, you will find it hard to gain back your capital.

Lack of Communication or Poor Communication

You have to make sure that you respond to your clients in a timely manner. If they have questions, you have to give them answers. If they give you feedback, you have to thank them, whether it is positive or negative. Remember that you can always learn from negative criticisms. You can use them to improve certain aspects of your business.

If you do it the right way, renting out equipment and tools can be highly profitable for you. You just have to determine the needs of the local market and make sure that you have enough funding for your equipment and tools.

You also have to come up with a good rental strategy in which you consider the key factors. Do not forget to consider if you would work with a rental company to manage the rental process for you. Hiring professionals with the right knowledge and experience can make your income stream even more profitable.

5. RENT OUT YOUR PARKING LOT

A parking lot or parking space is an interesting real estate investment. For example, in large cities such as San Francisco and New York, parking is at a premium. Individual spaces can even sell for more than $80,000.

If you cannot divide the parking space, you can sell it as a whole for at least $200,000. With this being said, you can conclude that parking spaces and parking lots are great money making opportunities. In fact, they are regularly listed at $300 to $400 monthly in San Francisco.

Say, the purchase price is $80,000 and the taxes are 1.5%. Your total expenses can reach $100 every month. If you can pull in $400 for rent, you can earn a monthly profit of $300. When you make $3,600 annually, you get a 4.5% return.

The Pros and Cons of Renting Out a Parking Lot

If you think that this amount is insignificant, you should consider the following advantages and disadvantages of investing in parking spaces or parking lots:

The Pros:

High Yields

In San Francisco, residential real estates yield less than 4.5%. So, you cannot purchase a condo unit for $800,000 and then rent it out to earn a monthly profit of $3,000. In this case, a parking space looks much better than a residential real estate property.

Low Entry Points

In many cities, the value of land is very high. Even though parking lots may not be financed, you may not be able to find anything that you can purchase for $400,000 even with an eighty percent loan to value ratio.

Not Management Intensive

Parking lots are not really management intensive. Unlike residential real estates, they do not need a lot of repairs. They are just there. If a customer stops paying for his parking space, you can simply have his vehicle towed.

Rent Control Avoidance

Rent control is a problem for a lot of landlords. You will not have this problem if you are just renting out a parking lot.

The Cons:

Increased Responsibility

Parking lots do not come without any risks. Just like any other business venture, you may also encounter some issues. For instance, you may need to have a lot of parking spaces in order for you to make enough money. This entails more responsibility. You have to be prepared for any problem that might arise.

Negative Perception On On-Site Parking and Car Ownership

In addition, on-demand car services and self-driving cars may change the way people view on-site parking and car ownership. This can significantly affect your business. So, you have to come up with a good strategy as well as backup plans.

Can Be a Hassle

If access to your parking space is restricted, you may have to be available to give your customers entry. Also, you will not be able to use your own parking space if you need it and someone else is renting it. You also have to constantly monitor the bookings as well as respond to queries.

Possible Legal Restrictions

Of course, you also have to consider the legal restrictions in your area. Find out if you can legally rent out your parking space to other people. See to it that you also submit necessary documents.

The Basic Principles behind Renting Out Parking Lots

In essence, you make money by renting out parking spaces or lots that you under-utilize or do not utilize at all. Your target market includes individuals who are in search of a secure and guaranteed parking for their vehicles.

You can actually rent out your driveway, garage, lock-up, off-street parking space, or even an empty plot of land. You can rent out any available space, provided that it is suitable for parking.

Why Would Anyone Be Willing to Rent Your Parking Space or Driveway?

The idea behind this money making opportunity may seem weird to some people, but renting out garages and driveways is actually not that uncommon.

In fact, a lot of employees want to conveniently park their cars near their workplace. Those who commute also want to park their cars near a train, coach, or tube station.

There are also lots of spectators who want to park near entertainment venues. People who travel often also want to park near the airport at a reduced rate. Many car owners also want to avoid the parking restrictions where they live.

Moreover, most tourists want to park near attractions. So, if you live near tourist spots, this is great news. Those who are visiting your town may also need an overnight parking spot.

6. RENT OUT YOUR FARM

Renting out a farm can be highly profitable. In fact, famous businessman Warren Buffett invested in a farm at the start of his business. He rented out farm land to farmers and earned a passive income.

What Makes Farms Attractive Investments?

Unlike technology, land never becomes outdated and obsolete. Decades and even centuries may pass, and land would still be valuable. They appreciate over time. Gadgets, such as computers, tablets, and mobile phones, on the other hand, decrease in value every year.

If you invest in a farm land, you can pass it down to your descendants. Unlike money market investments and stock options, you can also enjoy the use of your land even if you do not wait for the interest to grow.

Buying the Property

Depending on your location, the prices of farm lands may vary. In places where these properties are quite inexpensive, you can buy them for around $10,000 per acre.

This is great because you do not have to spend a lot of money on something valuable. You can even build a house there if you want.

How Much Farm Land Can You Rent Out?

Jim Ochterski from Cornell University said that property owners may charge about four percent of the value of their land to local farmers. This percentage would cover their property taxes, insurance, and profits.

Potential for Growth

Having a farm land may not seem like a huge deal now, but you should think long term. In the future, the population will increase in nearby towns and there would be more demand in products, supplies, and other things.

You can take advantage of this situation and make money by renting out your property. If nearby cities are expanding into your rural area or if the real estate market is high, your farm land can significantly increase in value. It can even be a great shield against inflation.

If you keep your money in a bank account that does not yield any interest, your purchasing power would decrease as the prices for commodities rise. On the other hand, if you own a property such as a farm land, your purchasing power stays the same. After all, the value of land goes up along with the value of commodities.

Tax Implications

Renting out a farm land also comes with certain tax implications that you have to be aware of.

Cash Rent Lease

With this option, the tenant has to pay a certain amount to the land-lord. This amount would depend on how many acres of farm land he is renting. Since you own the farm land, the payment you receive will be classified under rental income.

This is not subject to self-employment tax. However, you also have certain limitations when it comes to tax breaks. For instance, you cannot qualify for farm income averaging, expense deduction, special rule for estimated tax payments, and deduction for soil and water conservation expenses.

Crop Share Lease

This one is essentially an arrangement in which you agree to rent out your farm land to a tenant in exchange for crop shares. Your tax treatment of income, however, would depend on your level of participation in the farming activities. If you materially participate under the lease, your income would be subject to self-employment tax.

How Much Money Can You Earn?

The amount you can earn depends on the kind of property you have and to who you choose to rent out your farm land to. For example, if you rent out your property to hunters, you can earn around $4,000 per season.

Providing hunters a hunting ground can be good for your finances. If you have ponds in your area, you can expect animals to go there to drink. Deer, pronghorn antelopes, and doves will frequent your land.

What are the Possible Drawbacks?

When you rent out to hunters, you have to watch out for stray bullets. You also have to be prepared for any issue that might arise. For example, hunters may engage in fights with other hunters over animals.

There could be drunken fights, sub-leasing without your permission, poaching, and garbage piles as well. You have to be physically, mentally, and emotionally prepared for these kinds of problems.

What Should You Do?

You need to make sure that you have a well-defined contract. You and your clients should have clear expectations. John Devney, the Delta Waterfowl Foundation vice president, talked about horror stories in which both parties did not have clear expectations, causing them to end up in complex situations.

Devney recommends spelling out everything that you expect in your contract. This way, you can easily and quickly deal with any flaws. See to it that you also consider the needs of hunters, such as duck blinds and other structures. If you want to earn a decent sum of money, your land has to be an ideal place for wildlife. You also have to manage it properly.

You also have to network with your local hunters so that you can get a sense of the market. Ask these people to assess your farm land. You may also use the Internet to search for guidelines and contract samples from reliable and trusted sources.

If you are not confident with your own skills, you can seek help from experts. For example, you can contact the Hunting Lease Network. It is a company that charges twenty-five percent of the lease amount in exchange of evaluating the property and taking care of marketing.

They would deal with the negotiations and lease management for you. They would also disburse and collect payments as well as set rules for boundaries and access. They would also answer the queries that hunters may have and give them identification cards.

When working with companies like this, see to it that you also receive a liability insurance policy. After all, you cannot be completely sure that no one is going to get injured on your property.

7. NETWORK MARKETING

Marketing or promoting ads across the Internet is another great way to earn a passive income. You can take advantage of blogs and social media platforms among other resources.

Network Marketing via Facebook

Facebook, for instance, is a massive and highly influential social media platform with millions of users from all over the world. It allows you to interact and communicate with family, friends, colleagues, and even random strangers online. So, you can say that it is ideal for network marketing.

Network marketing is actually a very common way to make money on the site. However, you need to sign up with an affiliate before you can start promoting products or services via Facebook ads. Each time a user from your page lands onto the site of your affiliate merchant, you earn a commission or a percentage of the sales he makes.

You have to attract a lot of potential customers if you want to make more money. You can create a fan page that appeals to users. See to it that you post updates on a regular basis to keep them interested. Encourage them to like, share, and comment on the posts you create. Encourage them to make these posts viral on social media.

You can even use your personal account to advertise the goods of your affiliate merchant. You can share posts from your fan page so that your Facebook friends can see what you have to offer. If you are using Facebook as a selling platform, you can communicate with your customers via comments or personal message. Since Facebook does not really have a payment system, you can use online banking, wire transfer, or PayPal as your payment method.

Network Marketing via Blogs

Blogging is a great way to talk about anything and everything under the sun. You can use your blog to speak out your mind and share your ideas and experiences. You can elaborate on many other interesting things.

You can also use your blog as an online journal and talk about the details of your personal life. You can include pictures, music, and videos for added effect, and even have the option to reveal your identity or remain anonymous.

Since blogs are all over the Internet, you can attract the attention of millions of people. You can take advantage of the Web traffic that you generate to make money and then convert your readers into paying customers.

You can incorporate network marketing with blogging. As you know, you have to team up with an online merchant and get paid for endorsing his products or services. You earn either a fixed amount or a commission. You have to put ads on your blogs. Once your visitors click on these ads, they would be directed to the online store or page of the online merchant.

If you are still unsure of what to do, here are a couple of guidelines that you can follow:

a. Generate enough amounts of traffic

Online money making opportunities are mostly about the Web traffic. This is especially true for network marketing and blogging. It does not matter how interesting or informative your blog is. If you are not able to generate sufficient amounts of traffic, you will not earn money.

Search engine optimization is highly effective in generating traffic.

Users typically use these search engines to find what they are looking for. If your blog appears at the top of the search results, you have a better chance of being found than other websites.

To make the most of search engine optimization, you have to use the right keywords and key phrases. Do your research and find out which ones are trending at the moment.

You should also choose the ones that do not have a lot of competition. This way, you can take over this particular category. Experts recommend doing a research on the most popular keywords and then optimizing your blog to target such keywords.

A good website is quick to load. Online users are a very impatient kind. They do not like anything that loads slowly. So, when they get to your blog and it does not load within a few seconds, they will get bored immediately. They will leave your site.

Refrain from using link spams. These things are not helpful at all. They will not make your blog rank higher on the search engines. In fact, they may even hurt your ranking. Once the search engines detect spams on your blog, it can get blocked.

Of course, you should only post relevant content. Be specific and clear with what you want to say to avoid losing potential sales. You should also provide useful, helpful, and interesting content that readers will be prompted to share on their social media accounts.

b. Use social media platforms other than Facebook

Facebook is not the only social media platform that you can use. There are lots of other equally useful and attractive platforms, such as Twitter. You can also use Instagram, Pinterest, and Google Plus among others.

Social media networks are ubiquitous, and nearly every person has an account. You can take advantage of social media interaction to earn money. Just like with Facebook, you can use your Twitter to buy ads if you want to target a specific audience. Do not forget to use high quality images, compelling headlines, and a strong call to action.

You will surely find people who have the same interests as you. Just continue giving them what they want to keep them around. You can gain more followers if you post trending content. So, you should keep an eye out on what is trending by looking at the most used hashtags.

Do not forget to include a description and a URL link that redirects to your blog or website. This technique works well with network marketing. You can sign up with different affiliate marketing companies and select a product or service that you want to promote. Then, you can create blog entries and landing pages relevant to it.

Network Marketing via Twitter

With Twitter, earning money is not really the most difficult part. It is, in fact, building a network and accumulating followers. Attracting followers in the first place is already a struggle. Keeping them around is much more difficult. You have to be strategic about creating a plan on how to keep them enticed.

To attract the attention of your target audience, you have to show that you personally want to get to know them better. Aside from providing valuable content, you have to reply to their tweets, follow them back, and engage with them by discussing topics, inviting them to events or giving away contest prizes.

You can also post sponsored tweets that are paid for by advertisers, provided that you have a massive following. Big name companies will contact you if they see that you have a strong influence on social media.

There has to be a lot of engagement going on in your account. At this rate, even negative publicity can work in your favor. The world of social media is all about popularity. The more followers you have, the better your chances at getting a sponsorship.

You can also search for new leads. You can use Twitter's own search engine tool to find new customers based on their tweets and bios. Say, your affiliate merchant is in the business of selling custom desk calendars. You can type in keywords like "custom desk calendars" or "desk calendars", and you will see public tweets about these topics.

The users who tweeted them are likely going to be interested in your affiliate merchant's products. Connect with them by replying to their tweets. Then, entice them with coupons or promos.

Networking via Instagram

You can be part of a multilevel marketing company and build a team of network marketers. Since Instagram has millions of users, it is an ideal platform for displaying visual content. You can advertise the products or services of the merchants you are affiliated with on your own Instagram account.

Networking via Instagram involves the use of trackable links or promo codes that help convert clicks into sales. For example, if you are partners with a company that manufactures hair vitamins, you can post pictures of yourself using their products. You can also post selfies that show your healthy and vibrant hair.

Do not forget to include the URL's or product links in your bio. Instagram only allows links to be posted on the bio. Thus, you cannot promote multiple products all at the same time.

You can use a URL shortener if you want. You can also use promo codes as your affiliate links and insert these codes into your posts. You may also include the contact details of the company so that your followers can get in touch with them for queries.

Network Marketing via E-Mail

With e-mail marketing, you need to have a mailing list that contains the e-mail addresses of subscribers. Always remember that you have to update your subscribers regularly. Inform them about the latest happenings on your website.

E-mail marketing is all about making sales through e-mail. Do not think that this method is already outdated. To this day, people still receive e-mails from affiliate marketers with regard to various products and services.

E-mail marketing is not spam mail. It is also not the same as pyramid marketing, although it can be a form of network marketing. Nevertheless, it is a legitimate way to make money.

Keep in mind that effective e-mail marketing speaks to the general or specific interests of the receivers. Thus, when you send an e-mail to a subscriber, you have to make sure that it is interesting or helpful. Its receiver should obtain something valuable from it.

You also have to give your subscribers what they want. For example, if they signed up because of skin care products, you only have to send them e-mails regarding skin care products such as lotions, moisturizers, and toners. If you do not deliver your promise, they might lose interest in you.

In addition, you have to take note that good e-mail marketing gives subscribers an option to stop receiving e-mails. They should be free to come and go as they please. If they no longer want to get your e-mails, they should be able to unsubscribe at any time. You should not force them to stay subscribed to your mailing list.

It is easier to personalize e-mail marketing than any other marketing strategies. For example, you can show the first and last names of your newsletter subscribers. Also, you can use the e-mail as a direct connection between your subscribers and yourself rather than using something from your website.

Ideally, you should send personalized e-mails to new recruits. Each one of your subscribers should see that you are available and accessible. Keep in mind that your personal and professional relationships with your subscribers are much more important than the size of your mailing list.

It is pointless to have a massive mailing list if the people in it do not really care about anything you send. You will only waste time and energy if they keep ignoring your messages. On the other hand, it is great to have a small mailing list wherein every subscriber is interested in what is going with you or your business.

You can have a separate mailing list for different types of audience. Every one of your subscribers must receive a separate series of e-mails. Take note that your success depends on your mailing list. See to it that you make legitimate e-mail lists that consist of subscribers who wish to know more of what you offer.

How Can You Earn Money from Mailing Lists?

The following are the most common ways on how you can earn money through your mailing lists:

1. Affiliate Offers

Most people do not care about affiliate offers, so avoid sending direct ones. Instead, you should do reviews on the products and then upload your reviews on your website. Do not forget to mention how these products helped you in one way or another. Make sure that all your posts contain clickable URLs.

2. Products and Services

If you are offering certain products or services, you can send free reports and videos to your subscribers. This should be enough to capture their attention and keep them hooked. Then, you can introduce them to your training program, products, or services.

3. Subscriber Referral

You can also make money by redirecting your subscribers to certain websites. There are companies that pay people to refer subscribers to their websites so that they can check out their products. You can earn a commission for every subscriber that ends up downloading something from such website.

4. Ad Sponsorship

You can feature paragraphs that advertise sponsors to your e-mails. Make sure that you include the links to these sponsored ads. Depending on how big your mailing list is, you can earn as much as $100 or perhaps even more.

5. Thank You Pages

Whenever new subscribers sign up for your mailing list, you should send them thank you pages that request them to read your message and verify their subscription.

More Important Pointers

The attention span of people just keeps getting weaker over time. So, if you want to maintain your followers and prevent them from leaving you, make sure that they are happy and satisfied with your services.

Here are some more pointers to help you out:

a. Outsource content

Blogging is a nice hobby. It can help you alleviate stress and tension, not to mention, a good source of passive income. To maintain your credibility, see to it that you remain consistent throughout your blog.

However, if things start to get too overwhelming for you, you can get some help. You may outsource some content to help you save time and energy. You can also find stock images, videos, and even articles online. You can use them, as long as they are not copyrighted. You may also hire someone else to write your notes and feature other bloggers on your blog.

b. Use an auto responder to automate your sales

List building and e-mail marketing are highly profitable, which is why they have to be taken seriously. Do not destroy your own reputation by sending junk mail or spam.

Nobody wants to see spam messages in their inbox. If you send spam to your subscribers, they will most likely lose trust in you and never read your messages again. This is why you have to choose your emails carefully and know when you can send them.

Aside from content relevance and quality, timing is also crucial. Ideally, you should send messages when there are lots of traffic online. You should refrain from sending messages in the middle of the night or at the wee hours of the morning. Send your messages during times when people are likely to be on their computers or mobile device. This way, they can quickly read your messages.

You may also consider investing in an auto responder to manage your e-mails more effectively. You can use incentives such as info-products to attract the attention of your visitors. Once they confirm their subscription, your auto responder will start sending e-mails.

Make sure that you have an equal amount of promotional and informative messages in your auto responder. This way, your readers will not think that all you care about is marketing and making money.

c. Find and hire a community manager

Another way to save time is to find and hire a community manager. Moderating comments and social media accounts can take a lot of your time and energy. With a community manager, you can quickly engage with your target audience, come up with content, and create reports that show how much your returns on investments are.

Ideally, you should select someone who has enough experience in doing this task. Also, you should only work with people who are trustworthy, skilled, and capable of making a business grow..

8. BECOME A SILENT BUSINESS PARTNER

Funds are necessary to begin operating a small business. A lot of small business owners use their personal money to start their business. Some of them, however, search for active partners who can invest and help operate the business. Others opt for silent partners who merely invest money into the business but do not deal with daily operations.

The Difference between a Silent Investor and a Silent Partner

There are cases wherein a silent investor becomes different from a silent partner. For example, a silent partner may be a partial owner of the business while a silent investor may only provide capital and not own a percentage of the business.

A silent investor actually has more things in common with an angel investor. Just like angel investors, silent investors provide the money necessary to run a business. However, they do not have any right to manage the business. They are also not responsible for the debts that the company may incur.

On the other hand, silent partners are actually full business partners. They are just as responsible for any debts that the company may incur as the general partners, even though they are not the ones running it.

What are the Pros to Becoming a Silent Business Partner?

If you choose to become a silent business partner, you can enjoy the following benefits:

Passive Income

Since you are an investor, you get to receive your share from the business on a regular basis. You earn money even if you do not meddle with the operations. The amount of money you earn, however, depends on the status of the business. If it does well, you also earn well.

In addition, you have to consider the arrangement that you have made with the other partners of the business. For instance, the active partners may receive a bigger share than you since they actively participate in the operations of the business. Aside from money, they also spend time and energy. So, they do deserve to earn more money than someone who merely spends money.

Fewer Responsibilities

Startups usually require lots of work. Those who are involved in it need to endure long periods of labor and uncertainty. The active partners have to spend a significant amount of time to get the business up and running. Also, they have to make important decisions and deal with challenging situations. They may have to hire and terminate workers among other duties.

Since you are a silent partner, you do not have to do any of these tasks. You have fewer responsibilities, so you will not experience a lot of stress. You also have more free time since you do not have to be physically present in all of the meetings and operations.

Easier Investments

If you are an active partner, you have to work hard and ensure that the business succeeds. You have to study the market and do your research. You need to have sufficient knowledge and understanding of your industry. However, you are a silent partner. So, it is alright if you do not have a deep knowledge about everything. You can still invest in the business and simply wait for the results.

This gives you more time and freedom to select which investments you want to partake in. There is no need for you to limit yourself to areas or industries that you know.

Limited Liability

General partners usually invest resources and time in projects that might fail. This puts them at risk of having a mark on their record as well as being liable to stockholders and employees.

If you are a silent partner, your liability is limited. You may lose some resources and investments, but these are all that you will lose. You will not experience the stress and pressure that general partners will have in case something goes wrong and they have to face legal charges.

What are the Cons to Becoming a Silent Business Partner?

Just like with any other money making opportunity, becoming a silent business partner also has its share of downsides, such as the following:

Lack of Motivation

As a silent business partner, your role in the business is mostly to provide funding. This can be boring and discouraging for you, especially if you want to share your ideas and recommendations.

The general partners may listen to your input, but they do not really have to do what you want even though it is your money that they are spending.

No Input in Operations

You cannot control your investment because you agreed to a hands-off approach. You may offer some insights or give advice, but you cannot have a say with regard to implementation. The ultimate decisions would come from the general partners.

Over time, you may feel hurt that other people are running your business. You may also disagree with some of the decisions of the general partners. However, no matter how much you disagree with them, there is really nothing you can do. Your opinions do not have much value since you do not have any say with regard to the operations of the business.

How to Become a Silent Business Partner

If you want to become a silent business partner, you have to enter into a limited partnership agreement with a general partner. This other person is the one responsible for the daily operations of the business. He is the one who directly manages it and has a hands-on approach towards it.

See to it that you have a written partnership agreement. All the partners involved, whether general or silent, should have a copy of this agreement. All of you should also agree to the terms stated in it.

Discuss your expectations about the business. Clarifying things early on can help you avoid any future disagreements. See to it that you also talk about possible risks so that you can come up with backup plans and other business strategies.

Then, you have to formally register your limited partnership with the Secretary of State and the county clerk in which your business can be found. Keep in mind that you may be held liable for debts unless you form an LLP or a limited liability partnership.

Once you have registered, you have to apply for an EIN or Employer Identification Number. This would let you pay business taxes as well as help you get a business bank account.

9. OWN AN ATM MACHINE

Each time users use an ATM, they pay a fee of $2 to $3. Even though such amount seems nominal, they actually build up to a pretty huge sum. So, if you want to earn a passive income, owning an ATM is another great idea.

According to Favret Carriere Cronvich lawyer Paul Carriere, whenever a business lets an ATM to be placed in their area, they get a chance to earn a commission. Whenever a user makes a transaction using an ATM, he pays a surcharge.

Then again, those who own the business usually do not get the entire fee. When you rent an ATM, the business that maintains it would get some of the money. There may be a variety of split variations, but the business will always earn money depending on surcharge transactions.

It is true that businesses can earn a profit from the fees involved. Nevertheless, some people still search for ways on how to make money from using an ATM. Another way to make money with it is to run ads on it.

You can put a screen on top of your ATM and then sell ads to run it. This can boost your revenue significantly.

What are the Fees Involved?

Operating and owning an ATM is not free of charge. So, you have to make sure that you place your machine in a profitable location. You can either buy or rent one. As much as possible, you should buy the machine. Even though it is expensive, there is a huge chance for you to earn higher commissions for every surcharge transaction in the long run.

The costs of ATM's typically range from $1,000 to $10,000. Of course, this would depend on whether the machine is new or used. It is obviously less expensive to purchase a used machine. However, it may come with certain drawbacks, such as looking older and being slower. If people do not like the appearance and speed of your ATM, they may think that it is fraudulent and they may not use it anymore.

In addition, see to it that you consider certain vital factors when you purchase an ATM. For instance, you have to determine if you are going to buy a freestanding model or a counter-top model. The type of machine you choose can also affect its price.

Once you purchase an ATM, you become responsible for its mainte-nance. You have to keep it full of cash and ensure that it works properly. If you want to reduce your costs further, you can choose to eliminate the third party and load money into your ATM from your business. You can also place the ATM in a property that you own.

Owning an ATM can yield high profits. Fifteen to thirty transactions per month are enough to give you a decent sum of money. You can earn from $20,000 to $30,000 per year.

On the other hand, if you do not want to own the ATM because of the maintenance costs and services, you can simply engage in a full-ser-vice program. Here, the ATM would be maintained by the retailer. How-ever, this would also cost you money.

You also cannot place the ATM on your property. Instead, it would be placed in a retail location. So, you have to pay for the rent, which is usually a part of the service charge. It is also referred to as the commis-sion or rate of the retailer.

Starting an ATM Business for Passive Income

According to researchers, the ATM fees typically range from $1 to $8. For the past decade, these fees have increased at a significant rate. The fees are divided between partners or parties involved in the ATM ecosystem.

In general, the three parties involved are the owner, the processor, and the venue owner.

The owner of the ATM is you. You are the one who bought the machine and placed it in a certain location.

The venue owner is the individual that you have contacted for the place of your ATM. He receives the money that you pay for renting his property.

The processor is the organization or company that deals with the paperwork or processing of documents.

The fees collected from the ATM would then be divided among these parties. The processor contracts usually contain the terms, which are usually in a form of surcharge rebates and fees for every transaction.

The surcharge refers to the ATM fee or the amount necessary to make the ATM produce money. The surcharge rebate refers to the processor that refers to how much ATM fee gets returned.

You can expect a full return or 100% surcharge rebate on your charged fees. The ATM processors may also try to eat into the profits you make by adding network accessing fees or a percentage less than 100%.

The venue owner may earn $0.50 for every transaction. You can negotiate this amount. If the venue receives a lot of traffic, you may even offer half of the surcharge fee or ATM fee to the owner. After all, it will lead to a significant amount of fees.

You have to pay the venue owner and the ATM processor before you can get the remaining balance from the fees. The processor actually gets paid first and then the venue owner.

An Example to Help You Out

The average person withdraws $60 for every ATM transaction. So, you can expect your ATM to reach up to eight or ten transactions per day. This means that about $600 can be withdrawn each day.

The collected fees based on $3 for every transaction will eventually reach $24. If you pay your ATM processor $0.20 for every transaction, the fees involved would be $4. Then, $5.60 would be deducted from the fees and you will receive a gross profit of $18.40.

For the entire month, your gross profit can be $552. Your ATM can generate approximately $6,624 in gross profit per year.

What are the Pros of Owning an ATM Machine for Business?

For starters, an ATM business is pretty easy to maintain. Of course, you need to exert a considerable amount of effort in the beginning. Afterwards, however, you can let the business run on its own.

You can earn money from the service fees. You generate a passive income each time a person uses your machine.

What are the Cons of Owning an ATM Machine for Business?

For starters, you need to have enough funding to even start this kind of business. You need to have at least $5,000 to $10,000 to purchase the machine and fill it with cash.

If you plan to have more than one ATM machine, you need to have more funding. You also have to be willing to be on-call in case a problem arises with your ATM machines.

Ideally, you should live close to your machines so that you can attend to them right away. In case they need servicing, it would only take a few minutes for you to get there. The longer you leave a machine broken, the more profits you lose.

Furthermore, you need to choose the right location. Otherwise, you can lose more money than you make. You should place your machine in a spot where it will receive a lot of foot traffic, such as near office buildings and universities.

You may also want to choose a safe location. Avoid shady areas and neighborhoods.

When you understand the pros and cons to owning an ATM machine, you can better determine if this kind of business is right for you.

10. LICENSE YOUR PHOTOGRAPH

If you like photography and you have a whole stack of photos and generic ones, you can sell them online. Selling them as stock photos can help you collect payments without exerting any additional effort to promote them.

It is relatively easy to sell photos on various websites. However, you have to be persistent if you want to make good money out of it. A lot of other people are also into selling stock photos. You have to do your best to outdo them. See to it that you copyright your images so that other users cannot copy and use them without your permission.

Stock photos are pictures that can be licensed and arranged for specific purposes. They are typically used by those who need generic or specific photos for magazines, websites, brochures, graphic designs, web designs, and other purposes. A lot of business owners prefer stock photos for their projects and advertisements because they are cheaper and effective as regular ads.

With stock photos, there is no more need to hire a photographer and spend on other related expenses. It also helps them save time since they no longer have to schedule photo shoots or have meetings with the photographer.

You can also choose to host a portfolio of photos on your own website. Here, you can allow users to download your photos for free. Just make sure that you also restrict certain items.

If you know people who might be interested in stock photography, you can contact them directly and sell them your work. If they like your photos, you can create a gallery and have them as your private clients.

Likewise, if you know businesses that produce merchandise and goods such as shirts, calendars, and cups, you can offer them your photos. These photos will be printed on these items.

How Much Money Can You Earn with Stock Photos?

It really depends on how many photos you produce and what websites you go to. If you sell your work through subscriptions, you may only get paid for every download. Over time, however, such prices may increase.

If you want to earn more money, you should choose companies that pay more for photos that get frequently downloaded. You can also make a deal with the company to be exclusive. They can have exclusive access to your photos for a price.

For example, iStockphoto pays three times higher commissions to photographers who are exclusive with the company. Likewise, Dramstime gives bonuses to their exclusive photographers.

Keep in mind that some stock photography websites also have a minimum amount requirement. For instance, you have to reach $50 or $100 first if you want to withdraw your earnings. If your earnings are below the minimum amount, you will not be able to enjoy your profits.

Being a photographer is a cool profession. However, it may not always be profitable, especially during the low season. If this is the case, you have to find other ways on how to earn money.

You can check out the licensing market. You will be glad to know that your photos are in demand by advertisers, publishers, business owners, web designers, and graphic designers.

You can submit your photos online and earn money from them. There are plenty of stock photography websites that sell the rights for photographs to publishers and designers. These photos are then used in blog posts, book covers, and advertisements among others.

The Different Licensing Models

Royalty Free

You can go for the royalty free licensing model if you want to sell the rights to your photographs to multiple buyers and have little to no restrictions when it comes to the terms of use.

This means that your photos may be sold on various stock websites. The great thing with this option is that your work can be represented by huge and popular websites. Hence, you can have a better chance of selling your photos over and over again.

As much as possible, you should go for images that are generic and commonly used. For example, you can take photos of men and women in corporate attire, flowers, insects, children, and landscapes. These kinds of images are often used on business websites, greeting cards, product packaging, etc.

Once the buyer pays for the rights to use your photos, he is able to use it repeatedly as he wishes. Your photos can be placed on reports and websites among other places.

The fees associated with these types of photos are usually small. Clients usually do not purchase the exclusive rights to use the images. A lot of photographers opt for this model because they can build a huge portfolio and sell more in-demand images. They can earn a steady income from their work.

Rights Managed

You can also go for rights managed licensing if you want your clients to purchase the exclusive rights to your photos. These photos can only be used for a specific purpose, in a specific location, and for a specific duration of time.

With this type of licensing, a lot of stock companies ask that photographers do not license represented work with other companies. They want to be able to track the usage of the photos.

For example, a client may want to buy the rights to a photo because he intends to use it for an album or book cover. The fees associated with this type of licensing are usually higher.

However, the amount of money you earn is also limited to how many clients bought your photos. In addition, selling your photos does not mean that you can never make money from them again.

Where Can You Sell Photos?

If you search online, you will surely find a wide variety of stock photography websites. Some of these companies will only represent photos on a royalty free basis while others would choose the rights managed set up. You may also find companies that combine both types.

When you sell your photos, see to it that you consider the model that you use. It has to fit your personal style and preferences. More importantly, you have to be comfortable with your photos being used.

Anyway, if you want to make money from your photos, here are some of the websites that you can check out and submit them to:

- shutterstock.com

- gettyimages.com

- almay.com

- stocksy.com

- istockphoto.com

- trevillion.com

- shutterstock.com

- dreamstime.com

- milim.com

- arcangel.com

A lot of stock photography companies pay photographers a commission for every photo sold. Some of them also pay a fixed amount while others divide the earnings equally with the photographer.

Steps on How to Submit Photos Online and Earn a Passive Income

A lot of companies, whether they work on a royalty free basis or a rights managed basis, have similar submission processes. The following are the steps that you have to take if you want to make money from your photos:

Step 1: Ensure that you are the rightful owner of the photos

You must have the necessary property releases and models. It may seem tedious and difficult to obtain signed agreements each time you use a recognizable person or property in a licensed photo. However, this step is important.

Step 2: Decide if you want to sell your photographs using the royalty free model or the rights managed model.

You may only sell your photos using one licensing model. Hence, you have to study both models carefully and determine which one is best for your wants and needs.

Step 3: Choose the stock photography company that has the best offers

Of course, you want to make money from your photos. So, you should go for a company that offers a decent amount of money to photographers. Be wary of those that offer very low commission rates as well as those that have really strict requirements with regard to selling your work.

See to it that you read the fine print and understand everything before you submit your photos.

Step 4: Have a backup plan

Your photos may not be immediately accepted by your first choice of company. Thus, you should have a backup company to send them to. Search the Internet for the best and most recommended companies.

If you have the time, you should also read the blog entries of photographers who have successfully submitted their work and earned money. Their experiences and insights would give you an idea on what you have to do to succeed in this venture.

Step 5: Be familiar with all the policies and requirements

Research about the companies that you plan to contact. Find out about their policies so that you can carefully plan your moves. Keep in mind that some companies have strict policies with regard to exclusivity.

For example, Shutterstock requires photographers to take and pass an exam about their policies. This way, they can be sure that the photographers truly know and understand their requirements.

There are also companies that have specific requirements with regard to colorspace and file formats. For instance, many of them only accept RGB and JPEG. They are also usually particular about the camera mega pixels and minimum size of file. In addition, they usually reject photos with any visible logo, editing, or trademark.

Step 6: Prepare your photos according to the requirements of the stock photography company.

See to it that you check out the naming, keywording, and sizing of your photos, and ensure that everything is exactly what the company wants.

Step 7: Sign up for an account on the official website of the stock photography company.

You may need to sign up and create an account to be able to access the features of the website, such as contacting the team and uploading photos. Then again, this is not necessary for all websites. Some companies may simply ask you to e-mail your work or send them via file transfer.

Step 8: Work as a contributor and upload the photos that you want the stock photography company to consider

Prepare your portfolio of stock photography. It should showcase your best work. See to it that it is diverse and features a variety of genres. Submit your portfolio to the company along with your submission form.

Step 9: Review the terms and conditions of the stock photography company

Once you get accepted, make sure that you read the terms and conditions thoroughly. You need to understand everything that is included in the contract. If you see anything that you do not agree with, you may not sign the contract. Otherwise, you may continue and sign it.

Step 10: Expand your portfolio

If you want to continue making money from stock photos, you have to continue taking pictures and submitting them to companies. Watch the market and stay updated on the latest trends. Find out what clients want and give it to them.

The Pros and Cons of Selling Licensed Photographs Online

Just like everything else, there are positive and negative sides to this passive income opportunity.

The Pros:

Great Way to Supplement Income

You can turn your hobby into a money making opportunity. Simply take good photos, search for reputable stock photography companies, and make a submission. When you get accepted, you can earn a decent amount of money.

It Can Build Your Portfolio

You may not realize it immediately, but taking photos and selling them may be your most profitable talent. It can even be a stepping stone towards better things and greater deals. In the future, you can use your portfolio to start a business or get a job that is relevant to photography.

Continuous Royalties

You can still earn royalties for photos that you have taken many years ago. You can also earn money every time your licensing agreement is renewed. This is great because once your photos become viral, you can have a greater chance of earning more money.

The Cons:

Highly Competitive Market

These days, more and more people are venturing into stock photography. They have realized that taking random photos and selling them online to be used on websites, articles, covers, and other things is profitable.

So, when you try to submit your photos, you will see millions of them ahead of you. This may discourage you if you do not believe enough in your skills. Nonetheless, you should still go ahead and submit anyway.

Not Enough Earnings

If you do not choose where you submit your photos carefully, you may not be able to make enough money. This is why you always have to find as many options as possible. Then, you have to compare your choices and go for the one that has the best offer.

CONCLUSION

I'd like to thank you and congratulate you for transiting my lines from start to finish.

I hope this book was able to help you learn about the different types of income, as well as their advantages and disadvantages. I also hope that you were able to realize why passive income is the most attractive type of income.

With this new understanding, I hope that you were able to improve your financial status as well as the quality of your life. I also hope that you were able to expand your horizons and have a more open mind, especially when it comes to thinking of the right money-making opportunity for you.

As you know, nothing is completely guaranteed in life. Even the tips included in this book will not guarantee your success. Nevertheless, they can greatly help improve your odds of making the right decisions and minimizing errors.

Also, I hope that you have learned about the fundamentals of earning a passive income through the methods discussed in this book. I suggest that you try them out and explore all available options to find out if they work for you. Do your best and never give up.

The next step is to apply what you have learned from this book. Always practice what you preach as well. So, if you share your knowledge with family or friends, see to it that you also live up to their expectations by actually having a passive income source of your own.

I wish you the best of luck!

Made in the USA
Monee, IL
03 January 2021